Working and Writing for Change

Working and Writing for Change

Series Editors: Steve Parks and Jessica Pauszek
Associate Editor: Justin Lewis

The Working and Writing for Change series began during the 100th anniversary celebrations of NCTE. It was designed to recognize the collective work of teachers of English, Writing, Composition, and Rhetoric to work within and across diverse identities to ensure the field recognize and respect language, educational, political, and social rights of all students, teachers, and community members. While initially solely focused on the work of NCTE/CCCC Special Interest Groups and Caucuses, the series now includes texts written by individuals in partnership with other communities struggling for social recognition and justice.

Recent Books in the Series

Speaking Back: Student Voices from Writing and Tutoring across Cultures, ed. by Kate Kostelnik, Derek Cavens, Susan Gonzalez Guevara, Quenby Hersh, Hannah Loeb, and Casey Ocasal

UVA Untold: Black Women's Narratives at the University of Virginia, ed. by Cheyenne Butler

Communities in Action: Creating Spaces of Social Change, edited by Yndalecio Isaac Hinojosa, Isabel Baca, and Jasmine Villa

The People Demand Democracy: Voices from the Myanmar Spring Revolution, ed. by Pratha Purushottam, et al.

A Parent's POWER by Sylvia P. Simms

The Forever Colony by Victor Villanueva

Visibly (and Invisibly) Muslin on Grounds: Classroom, Culture, and Community at the University of Virginia, ed. by Wafa Salah and Fawzia Tahsin

The Lived Experience of Democracy: Criticizing Injustice, Building Community, ed. by Kaitlyn Baker, et al.

Steal the Street: The Intersection of Homelessness and Gentrification by Mark Mussman

Literacy and Pedagogy in an Age of Misinformation and Disinformation ed. by Tara Lockhart, Brenda Glascott, Chris Warnick, Juli Parrish, & Justin Lewis

Faces of Courage: Ten Years of Building Sanctuary by Harvey Finkle

Equality and Justice: An Engaged Generation, a Troubled World by Michael Chehade, Alex Granner, Ahmed Abdelhakim Hachelaf, Madhu Napa, Samantha Owens, & Steve Parks

Other People's English: Code-Meshing, Code-Switching, and African American Literacy by Vershawn Ashanti Young, Rusty Barrett, Y'Shanda Young-Rivera, & Kim Brian Lovejoy

Becoming International: Musings on Studying Abroad in America, ed.by Sadie Shorr-Parks

Dreams and Nightmares: I Fled Alone to the United States When I Was Fourteen by Liliana Velásquez. ed. and trans. by Mark Lyon

The Weight of My Armor: Creative Nonfiction and Poetry by the Syracuse Veterans' Writing Group, ed. by Ivy Kleinbart, Peter McShane, & Eileen Schell

PHD to PhD: How Education Saved My Life by Elaine Richardson

Speaking Back:
Student Voices from Writing and Tutoring across Cultures

Edited by

Kate Kostelnik, Derek Cavens,
Susan Gonzalez Guevara, Quenby Hersh,
Hannah Loeb, and Casey Ocasal

Parlor Press
Anderson, South Carolina
www.parlorpress.com

Parlor Press LLC, Anderson, South Carolina, USA
Copyright © 2025 by New City Community Press.

No part of this book may be reproduced or transmitted in any form, by any means electronic or mechanical, including photocopying and recording, or by any information storage or retrieval system, without written permission from the publisher. Printed in the United States of America on acid-free paper.

Library of Congress Cataloging-in-Publication Data on File

1 2 3 4 5

978-1-64317-541-6 (paperback)
978-1-64317-542-3 (pdf)

Working and Writing for Change
A Parlor Press series.
Editors: Steve Parks and Jessica Pauszek

Book design by Justin Lewis // justinlewis.me
Cover illustration by Caitlin Gerrard

Parlor Press, LLC is an independent publisher of scholarly and trade titles in print and multimedia formats. This book is available in paper and eBook formats from Parlor Press on the World Wide Web at https://parlorpress.com or through on-line and brick-and-mortar bookstores. For submission information or to find out about Parlor Press publications, write to Parlor Press, 3015 Brackenberry Drive, Anderson, South Carolina, 29621, or email editor@parlorpress.com.

Contents

Acknowledgments   *vii*
   Kate Kostelnik

Introduction: Into Communities and Across Disciplines   *1*
   Kate Kostelnik

Part I: Into Communities

1 Fourteen Years' Difference   *15*
   Mariam Mohamed

2 Learning from Refugees   *26*
   Ahmed Mohamed

3 Fading Dreams: A Retrospective on American Education   *35*
   Thaqeb Chowdhury

4 The Way Through the Nostrils: An Attempt to Remember   *43*
   Caitlin Gerrard

Part II: Across Disciplines and Through a Pandemic

5 What Writing Center Studies Can Learn from Gender-Affirmative Psychotherapy   *54*
   Anonymous

6 Utilizing Writing Center Pedagogy to Improve Communication in Healthcare for Limited English Proficiency Patients   *67*
   Melissa Abel

7 From Speech Pathology to Writing Tutor   *77*
   Kirsty Thompson

8 The Negative Implications of Western-Centric Scientific Writing Guidelines and a Solution for Struggling Scientists   *93*
   Tanvika Vegiraju

9 Finding Power in Marginalization: Preserving Nurture in the Writing Center *103*
    Kaitlyn Baker

10 The Missing Lens: The Absence of Intersectionality in Education *117*
    Saoirse Farrell

11 Clara Luz *129*
    Susan Gonzalez Guevara

Contributor Biographies *139*

Acknowledgments
Kate Kostelnik

First, I would like to thank Dr. Kate Stephenson and Dr. Steve Parks for the opportunity—through funding from the Jefferson Trust—to publish this book. Dr. Stephenson and Dr. Parks, in addition to Dr. Tamika Carey, also led foundational professional development opportunities that introduced me to community-engaged course design. Along with Kate, Steve, and Tamika, many thanks also to my wonderful colleagues from the UVA Department of Writing and Rhetoric: Patricia Sullivan, Steph Ceraso, Anastatia Curley, Heidi Nobles, John Casteen, Marcus Meade, Sarah O'Brien, devin donovan, Victor Luftig, T. Kenny Fountain, Kevin Smith, Claire Chantell, Keith Driver, and Jim Seitz have supported me in scholarship, teaching, and life.

Students who helped at different points in the process, Quenby Hersh and Susan Gonzalez Guevara, did excellent work editing and selecting essays. Hannah Loeb—who also participated in "The Practice, Ethics, and Discipline of Community Partnerships Pedagogies," led by Steve Parks, Kate Stephenson, and Tamika Carey—would edit, coach writers through further revisions, and inspire me with her energy and talent. Also critical in the extensive edits and revisions, my husband, Derek Cavens, added extensive final edits in the summer of '23. Casey Ocasal would help with final edits in that fall. Diarra Dia also offered some strong feedback on the introduction.

I received additional support in continued professional development and conversations with the Provost for Academic Outreach, Louis Nelson, and Ellen Blackmon. In conjunction with Kate Stephenson—in her leadership of the Engaged Teaching Scholars—professors and community members in Charlottesville fortified my energy and commitment to experiential learning and community-engaged scholarship. I am thankful to Madison House and C4K (Computers 4 Kids), led by Kala Somerville and Tricia Howell, for creating partnerships and helping my students connect to community members. Prior to these partnerships, Keith Driver, leader of the Faculty Seminar on the Teaching of Writing '17, posed a meaningful question about course design: "Is this a tutoring course or a writing course?" A very good question that I still can't answer. Just as I'm simultaneously a creative writer, writing center scholar, antiracism activist, writing teacher, and advocate for community-engaged learning, it's not one or the other. I believe I can be many things as a professor, and my robust interdisciplinary courses can serve diverse students and community members seeking meaningful connections.

As a PhD candidate, I was fortunate to work with Bobbi Olson, Stacey Waite, Zachary Beare, Nicole Green, Travis Adams, Charise Alexander Adams, Aimee Allard, Marcus Meade, Kim Banion, Lupe Linares, Lindsay Mayo-Fincher, Chad Fincher, Clarence Harlan Orsi, Leslie Bartlett, Cody Lumpkin, Ashley Lawson Quatro, Erica Rogers, and last but certainly not least—Frankie Condon. These academics and friends didn't let me panic about not fitting into any one box as a compositionist, creative writer, or literature professor. Likewise, as this book argues, we need to let student writers choose their genres and rhetorical traditions, and that certainly means allowing for hybrid forms. As Condon continually emphasized, we are all writers, and writing centers can be more than a place to work on writing.

Thank you to tutors and students from Missoula, Montana; Edison, New Jersey; Lincoln, Nebraska; Chestertown, Maryland; and Charlottesville, Virginia.

I thank my family, Mike Kostelnik, Pam Kostelnik, David Kostelnik, Carol Toth, and Derek Cavens for supporting me. Of course, thank you to my daughter Hazel who is endlessly patient with her workaholic mother.

Finally, many thanks to New City Community Press for allowing me to publish a later version of "Fourteen Years' Difference" by Mariam Mohamed. An earlier version of this essay appears in *Democracy 2021*, edited by Kaitlyn Baker.

Introduction: Into Communities and Across Disciplines

Kate Kostelnik

> The expectation that writing centers should "fix" the English of international ESL students ties in with broader assumptions that privilege monolingual Euro-American viewpoints. Rather than accepting institutional forces geared to the maintenance of these viewpoints, however, writing center specialists can take a leadership role in promoting a more multicultural and multilingual worldview. In doing so, writing centers can help prepare the academy for the complex cultural, linguistic, and national negotiations with difference that characterize our increasingly globalized world.
>
> —Steven Bailey
> "Tutor Handbooks: Heuristic Texts for Negotiating Difference in a Globalized World," *Praxis*

Imagine university students putting their learning directly to work in the community. Imagine partnerships in which students collaborate with migrant workers learning English, refugees working on resumes, and underserved children in need of one-on-one attention. Yes, we should teach students to consider complex cultural, structural, and socio-economic issues, but what if we went beyond consideration? In "English Studies and Public Service," Thomas Deans writes, "we have entered a critical period in which colleges and universities need to *reimagine* not only how they go about teaching and doing research but also how they relate to both their host communities and society more generally" (101; emphasis added). Imagine students engaging with community members and putting experiences into conversations with theory and research in writing projects.

Technically, my course at the University of Virginia, "Writing and Tutoring Across Cultures" is a writing center practicum with an engaged learning[1] component where students work weekly with multilingual writers in the community and then design public-facing projects, but it's more like conducting an orchestra than teaching.

---

1. Engaged learning has been called "service learning" in the discourse, but you'll also see scholars use "community-based learning" or "community writing" to refer to courses with community-engaged components. See the discussion by Deans later in this essay for elaboration.

Students learn to do the work of advising writers as they draft, and often their coaching of one another proves more valuable than mine.

This collection showcases the writing of eleven students from five iterations of "Writing and Tutoring Across Cultures." In addition to tutoring techniques, intercultural communication, and an emphasis on helping writers grow—rather than just fixing writing—students learn about contrastive rhetorics,[2] world Englishes,[3] rhetorical listening,[4] and the translingual approach.[5] Students select various on-and-off-Grounds tutoring sites including LAMA (Latinx and Migrant Aid) and ESOL (English for Speakers of Other Languages) classes. While courses that combine writing center pedagogy and weekly experience in community settings are hardly innovative,[6] and community-engaged learning in college classrooms has been well-documented and theorized,[7] UVA students generally didn't have the opportunity to tutor in Charlottesville as a part of coursework. That changed after the infamous 2017 Summer of Hate. Claudrena Harold and Louis Nelson explain:

> [u]ntil August 11, 2017, the University of Virginia generally positioned itself as separate from the city. Faculty, staff, and some students understood themselves to be citizens of the city and participated in these conversations as individual activists, but the institution stood alongside the city disengaged. This policy of disengagement failed to safeguard the university from the rising tide of anti-Semitism, racism, and violence. In the dusk hours of August 11, hundreds of white nationalists gathered in a large open athletic field and prepared for a torch-lit march through Grounds to the iconic statue of Thomas Jefferson in the plaza in front of the university's Rotunda. The thin veil of distinction quickly dissolved. (11)

After that tumultuous summer, I sought to engage with a community that had been both recently attacked by white supremacists and historically disregarded—not to mention, in some cases, harmed—by the University of Virginia. As an employee of that university, I followed directive emails from the administration to stay away from the anticipated violence on August 12th and 13th. As the mother of a young child, I

---

2. Different cultures have various preferences in terms of organization, style, documentation, etc.
3. Different Englishes are used in different regions of the world. All are valid.
4. Rhetorical Listening, a trope for interpretive inventions defined by Krista Ratcliffe, entails listening for cultural and historical forces that shape communication.
5. This approach to writing, according to Horner et al., allows for code meshing between languages. Different languages are resources from which to draw.
6. See an example of a similar course in Anne E. Green's narrative in Davi, Angelique et al. "Exploring Difference in the Service-Learning Classroom: Three Teachers Write about Anger, Sexuality, and Social Justice." *Writing and Community Engagement*. Edited by Thomas Deans et al, Bedford, 2010, pp. 465-484.
7. See again Deans et al. *Writing and Community Engagement*, Bedford, 2010.

also worried about putting myself in danger. In "Why the Nazis Came to Charlottesville," cultural historian Siva Vaidhyanathan writes about feeling conflicted as a parent but regrets not doing more. He questions:

> Does my status as a parent make me special? It shouldn't. A young man named Dre Harris was ambushed in a parking lot and took dozens of blows by club-wielding thugs. He took them so I wouldn't have to. Next time I will stand on the street with my neighbors, even at the risk of injury or death. It's the least I can do to repay those who stood bravely this time.

Like my colleague, I couldn't take back my decision to leave town with my family that weekend, but I could teach, and my background and scholarship in Writing Center Studies provided a foundation in dialogical engagement. As an instructor of writing center practicums, I'd taught ethical collaboration with writers, so the move toward equitable community partnerships wasn't too far a stretch. I knew that responsible UVA students could be entrusted to do this kind of engagement.

To explain why I knew they were capable—and thereby to preface the essays of this collection—I need to backtrack even more, to before the summer of 2017, when I began working with UVA students in the fall of 2014. As a former graduate student and high school teacher of honors and AP classes, I'd worked with many strong, motivated students, but the learning culture at UVA seemed different. Students come from rural southern hollers, every exit off the beltway, all fifty states, and 147 countries. Admission is highly competitive, and, once enrolled, students compete for entry into majors, clubs, and distinguished majors' programs. They work very hard on academics, extracurriculars, and pre-professional training; some are also Division I athletes.

When attempting to describe UVA students' commitment and engagement, I defer to a colleague with forty years of experience at this university. Mark Edmundson writes:

> Our students love UVA for many reasons, but a chief one is that they feel it is *theirs*. . . . They govern themselves, they enforce their own code of honor, they participate in major decisions. As much probably as at any other institution, they influence the course of events."

In March of 2022, UVA students voted to make our honor code rehabilitative rather than punitive, and I would add that students thoughtfully and passionately respond to tragic events—like the racial profiling and brutalization of Martese Johnson in 2015 and, again, the Unite the Right rally of 2017—with inquiries, scholarship, and activism. Whatever happens, Grounds[8] is *theirs* to care for.

In fact, the culture is as caring as it is competitive. Yes, students vie with one another for grades, leadership positions, and spots in graduate programs; however, as much as they grapple, they also work for social justice and look after one another, especially when upperclassmen mentor first-years. It very well may be the case that only

---

8. The community refers to the campus as "Grounds."

UVA students truly understand their pressures and work ethics. I'd like to say that my first-year writing classes help new students acclimate to life on Grounds, but I'm certain—as evidenced by my students' writing—that mentoring programs like the Peer Advisors Program, through the Office of African American Affairs,[9] enable students to find their communities and join our larger one. And, of course, the writing center offers another space where students work with each other, specifically on writing and acclimating to academic discourses.

As a writing center administrator and instructor of writing center practicums that train potential tutors, I know that UVA students apply to be peer consultants because they want to help one another. Some know what it's like to attempt a ten-page research paper without the preparation and confidence that come from private SAT tutors and AP credit. Others have endured the humiliation of having their calculations checked by lab-mates. Many know how hard it is to contribute to class discussions when some classmates look sideways at southern and Mandarin accents. A great deal love writing but need help understanding that not all students have advantages like shelves of English books at home, well-trained instructors, and the time to practice and understand the process.

As a professor who creates writing classes in which students write for real audiences and serve larger enterprises—like writing culture, anti-racism, and linguistic justice—beyond their own learning, I was ready to set learning outcomes that reach beyond honing writing skills toward promoting social justice. I already employed course discussion forums as places for students to reflect on learning experiences and texts. In fact, I'd been emphasizing the importance of written reflection that Thomas Deans discusses in "English Studies and Public Service":

> The Commission on National and Community service defines service-learning as a method of teaching that a) provides educational experiences under which students learn and develop through participation in thoughtfully organized service experiences that meet community needs . . . ; b) is integrated into the students' academic curriculum or provides structured time for students to think, talk, or write about what the students saw and did . . . ; c) provides a student with opportunities to use newly acquired skills and knowledge in real-life situations in their own communities; and d) enhances what is taught in school by extending student learning beyond the classroom . . . . Thus service-learning is not volunteerism or community service . . . ; it is at heart a pedagogy of action and reflection, one that centers on a dialogic between community outreach and academic inquiry. (97–98)

In my course, "Writing and Tutoring Across Cultures," the course forum—our place of reflection where, as Deans puts it, students "write about what [they] saw and did"—would become a much more integral "living" text than in past writing courses. I

---

9. Williams, Sarah L. "The Peer Advisor Program. OAA.virginia.edu. UVA, 11 July 2022, https://oaaa.virginia.edu/peer-advisor-program-1989-2009

realized that students needed even more space and time to consider their community engagement in the context of course content. They also needed to flesh out ideas for public-facing final projects that would share their learning—the essays I'll shortly introduce.

But first, let me expand upon the forum discussions that laid the foundation for writing projects and provide a window into learning, collaboration, and activism. Instead of formal assignments early in the semester,[10] students wrote on a weekly discussion forum. Half the class would begin by writing (approximately) five-hundred-word posts where they might work through experiences, readings, and further thoughts on class discussions—basically, anything related to class. The rest of the class would respond to these posts. I will say that, as effective and engaging as full-class discussion can be, writing forums allow for more careful and democratic participation. Live in-class discussions often proceed with one or two students raising their hands to contribute; the conversation can be unfairly dominated by the instructor and eager students. The discussion board allows multiple students to answer questions, steer the conversation, and take the necessary time to produce thoughtful posts; it also levels the playing field for multilingual writers working through translation and new vocabularies.

This window into learning showcased students practicing tutoring techniques and fortifying their understanding of Writing Center Studies scholarship. Forum posts also let the rest of us benefit from their experience with the broader community. One semester, a student wrote about helping a Turkish man navigate an automated phone message from a hospital and make a doctor's appointment. A pre-med student used tutoring techniques to work with a stroke patient during her volunteer work at the University hospital. Another pre-med student wrote about the challenge of trying to help her tutee translate Spanish into English when the tutee could neither read nor write in his native tongue. On the forum, her classmates and I brainstormed strategies that went beyond writing center pedagogy.

Part I: Into Communities

In the fall of 2019, Mariam Mohamed worked with a third grader named Nour,[11] who wore a hijab. Mariam, also a hijabi, would write forum posts about a very sleepy but strong student who liked to break up tutoring sessions with games of one-on-one basketball.[12] Mariam learned that Nour had behavior issues and frequently experienced meltdowns during the regular school day. Teachers couldn't communi-

---

10. There are traditionally three larger writing projects in most writing classes.
11. Nour is a pseudonym. Names of the tutees in this collection have been changed.
12. This was a go-to activity for many tutors working with younger writers. When tutoring college-level writers, tutors will often take their tutees for a walk when sessions get stressful, or the writer needs a break. Tutors frequently discussed these kinds of adaptations on the discussion forums.

cate with Nour's Swahili-speaking mother, but Mariam would learn that the girl was exhausted from caring for her young siblings, and she was frustrated by having to mind both her parents and her teachers. Also on the forum, Mariam would connect memories of her own difficult experiences in ESL classrooms as well as the bullying her brother endured when her own family first arrived in Brooklyn from Egypt.

The discussion forum could be an intimate space in which writers, like Mariam, shared their mis-educations—moves that they would not replicate with their tutees. When introduced to the concept of reading multilingual writers' texts with generosity rather than just searching for errors, many ESL program veterans also learned to be kinder when reading and revising their own texts. As per Horner et al's "Language Difference in Writing: Toward a Translingual Approach," students came to see language difference "not as a barrier to overcome or a problem to manage, but as a resource for producing meaning in writing, speaking, and listening" (303). Students who had avoided writing composed posts celebrating rhetorical moves from their native languages—such as proverbs and eight-legged structures.

Forum posts offered us glimpses into new aspects of life in Charlottesville, strengthened our classroom community, and allowed students to plan for final projects. Towards the end of the semester, when students were working extensively on those projects, Mariam came to me to discuss her plans. The final assignment, which will be detailed in section two of this essay, asks students to use their learning to speak back to an audience of their choosing. Mariam had become comfortable writing to me and to other tutors with similar tutoring and learning experiences, and I told her that she could write about everything, explaining how her past informed her present; you will find her essay, "Fourteen Years' Difference," in this collection. However, back in December of 2019, Mariam worried that she didn't have the authority to tell her story in that context; she didn't think her own narrative was significant. I explained to Mariam that Writing Center Studies discourse welcomes experiences of student tutors and suggested that she re-read her forum posts, treating them as early drafts that would enable her to create something brave, honest, and important. Academics traditionally write about multilingual learning from a theoretical perspective, but here was her opportunity to speak back as a learner and tutor.

Ahmed Mohamed, Mariam's brother,[13] writes just as bravely. That next spring of 2020, Ahmed's forum posts explained his difficulties working with refugees[14] who spoke different Arabics. Ahmed speaks and writes fluent Egyptian Arabic, but his tutee, Musa, spoke Syrian Arabic. Ahmed's posts detailed dialogic engagement and rhetorical listening in the context of his tutoring. He would need another Arabic-speaking classmate to translate Musa's Syrian Arabic into Egyptian Arabic. Would this extra

---

13. Another wonderful aspect of working with caring, talented students, is that they recommend my classes to their caring, talented friends and siblings.

14. Ahmed worked with the International Rescue Committee of Charlottesville, https://www.rescue.org/united-states/charlottesville-va

step allow Ahmed to listen to Musa with proper intent? Krista Ratcliffe's theory of rhetorical listening asks listeners to consider historical and cultural contexts (209) that influence writers' choices; likewise, Ahmed worried about what was being lost in translation. In "Learning from Refugees," he would explain how course readings connected and disconnected with his experiences. Ahmed Mohamed's piece in this collection speaks back to scholarship, but I would argue that he's also doing other important work in repairing and uniting Arabic discourse communities. He connects speakers with speakers and dialects with dialects, bridging divides in a way that recalls Monica Hanna's "Reassembling the Fragments." Hanna argues that when you break a vase—or a culture—the fragments that get pressed together and glued are far stronger and more beautiful than the undamaged whole (498). Ahmed and Mariam Mohamed speak back to the troubled world with their projects. They generously share their backgrounds, as well as the lives of community members like Nour and Musa—stories that might otherwise have been lost.

The next essay, by Ahmed's classmate Thaqeb Chowdhury, "Fading Dreams: A Retrospective on American Education," explains the sacrifices and difficult choices second-generation students often make. Thaqeb details the pressures of competing with other students in high school, getting into a top university, and then securing a high paying finance job. His love for and obligation to his family forced him to defer his dream of becoming a writer. In our class, he would tutor younger writers at a Charlottesville non-profit called Computers for Kids (C4K), an organization that offers mentoring and access to technology for students on free-lunch programs. In this space, he would work with students without the pressure of grades or traditional educational structures. He writes about the real curiosity and connection he encountered in an environment so unlike his own schooling, where "classes stopped feeling like places of learning; instead, they became steppingstones to the next evaluation" (55). Thaqeb has since become a successful analyst, but he's a writer as well. Like so many of my students, he endured the rigors of traditional schooling, secured a competitive position, *and* kept writing in his life. Using writing to learn is something that will never fade.

In Caitlin Gerrard's essay, "The Way Through the Nostrils, an Attempt to Remember," she writes about tutoring adult ESL learners, re-learning Mandarin, studying English literature, *and* using both Eastern and Western rhetorics in her non-fiction writing. She code-meshes[15] Mandarin and English as a means of reconciling her Chinese identity with her English major. Weaving Mandarin characters, English words, and sensory experiences together, she tells the story of her mother's immigration, marriage, and eventual return to Shanghai. To be clear, my undergraduate editor, Susan Gonzalez Guevara, and I decided to invite multilingual submissions; we're aware Caitlin's meshing may be unlike anything many readers have ever encountered. Other readers will easily comprehend her code-meshing and emphasis on

---

15. This approach to communication sees all languages and dialects, or codes, as equal resources. Writers and speakers use multiple codes simultaneously. See Vershawn Young's "Nah We Straight".

Eastern roundness and community, as opposed to Western linearity and individuality. Furthermore, readers of this collection might pause when reading what they conceive as errors in subject-verb agreement and unfamiliar logic. Although all the texts went through several revision cycles and careful copy editing[16] by UVA English graduate students Quenby Hersh, Hannah Loeb, and Casey Ocasal to make this collection reader-based,[17] readers still might encounter moves, structures, and logics from other cultures. Some writers celebrate their multilingual identities by leaving accented English—what some English readers might see as errors—intact.

Part II. Across Disciplines and Through a Pandemic

And this brings me to the next section of essays focused on interdisciplinary inquiry. The final project assignment for the course instructs:

> In "The Novice as Expert," Sommers and Saltz discuss the importance for instructors to give "real intellectual tasks that allow students to bring their interests to the course" (140). Design and execute a writing project that will allow you to meet the following goals: bring your unique perspectives to the course; use course content (readings, forum posts, concepts, and best practices in Writing Center Studies); help you write to a larger purpose beyond this course; put forth original thinking; work on writing in which you are passionate (and that you might not be able to tackle in traditional coursework); and engage with academic work in your discipline.

While many students use narrative in their final projects, others striving for scholarly genres choose to inquire into what their major or academic area of study could borrow from Writing Center Studies and vice versa. In this collection, you'll find essays from students immersed in their disciplines and ready to make interdisciplinary connections.

Anonymous's "What Writing Center Studies Can Learn from Gender Affirmative Psychotherapy" considers how strengths-based pedagogies compare to current

---

16. It's quite ironic that the student-tutors had their work subjected to precise copy-editing. As tutors, they learn to read generously and prioritize errors that get in the way of what a writer is trying to say—rather than "fixing" everything and aiming for "standard English," but this book project is a different animal than the class. In "Guilt-Free Tutoring," Blau and Hall explain that "[a] colleague from the university, an accomplished scholar in her field, hails from Spain. She speaks with a foreign accent and writes with one as well. She says if she must produce letter perfect idiomatic English, she hires an editor" (25). While current scholarship, like *Linguistic Justice on Campus*, pushes against monolingualism and "standard American edited English," the editors and I decided to aim for reader-based prose.

17. Writer-based prose makes sense to the author, but reader-based prose has been revised for a reader to understand. See detailed explanation in Flower. These terms differ from writer-responsibility, meaning the writer is responsible for clear communication, and reader-responsibility, meaning the reader must make sense of the prose. See McCool for elaboration.

trends in therapy strategies for LGBTQ+ patients. Melissa Abel recounts applying tutoring techniques while volunteering in a hospital in "Utilizing Writing Center Pedagogy to Improve Communication in Healthcare for Limited English Proficiency Patients." Both Melissa and Anonymous chose to write about pre-professional training, and this focus might have had something to do with the fact that they weren't able to do community tutoring during Fall 2020 and Spring 2021, the pandemic semesters. In past iterations of the course, other students have written interdisciplinary projects. For example, in "From Speech Pathology to Writing Tutor," (originally drafted in 2019) Kirsty Thompson sees critical overlap in the way that speech therapists work with patients and tutors work with writers. In 2020, students executed more interdisciplinary projects during the pandemic semesters because they had little contact with the Charlottesville community.

During Covid, when class meeting and tutoring sessions were confined to Zoom, I arranged for my students to work with first-year and multilingual students. Tutor-tutee pairs met weekly to work on writing and adjusting to college life in these unprecedented and atypical semesters. In writing center work, it's ideal to build a relationship with a writer who regularly comes to the center. Nevertheless, these pairs connected and shared a great deal of writing; indeed, in many cases, Covid isolation made these relationships critical to students' well-being. For first-year and multilingual students who elected not to come to Grounds—mostly because they had to work to supplement family income, serve as caretakers for siblings and relatives, or were themselves immunocompromised—tutors were lifelines. UVA's caring culture would get us through the difficulties of learning during Covid.

In the fall of 2021, we returned to Grounds in masks, and, while many students returned to community sites for tutoring, I allowed students to elect to work with a first-year or multilingual student throughout the semester. In addition to drafting projects about community tutoring, students continued to consider interdisciplinary connections. Tanvika Vegiraju contributes "The Negative Implications of Western-Centric Scientific Writing Guidelines and a Solution for Struggling Scientists," and Kaitlyn Baker looks to the feminization of writing centers in "Finding Power in Marginalization: Preserving Nurture in the Writing Center."

Other students considered scholarship in the context of their experiences. Saoirse Farrell's "The Missing Lens: The Absence of Intersectionality in Education" considers Women's and Gender Studies texts and theories that contrast deeply with her learning and experiences in traditional Catholic schooling. In her essay, she also rhetorically listens to her own writing. With dual citizenship, Saoirse plans to eventually teach Women's and Gender Studies to high school students in both Ireland and the United States. Essays in this collection consider how our pasts as writers affect our present as tutors, detail community engagement, contribute to scholarship, and move between disciplines. Scholarship and narratives offer windows into the lives and training of rising professionals.

The final essay in this collection, Susan Gonzalez Guevara's "Clara Luz," recovers a history that might have been lost had she not mustered the courage to write it. Clara Luz, Susan's mother from Guatemala, hadn't been able to access education in either her native country or in Virginia after immigrating as an adult. Susan translates and illuminates the story of a woman who risked everything for her children and then continued to care for extended family in Alexandria, Virginia. Susan also sacrificed living on campus for her first semester in fall 2020; she attended online classes, cared for her cousins, and continued working to contribute to the family. In our course that following fall, Susan would volunteer with Spanish speakers studying for the GED at Sin Barreras, helping other immigrants find brighter futures. As an English professor, I'm awestruck by what students can do on the page and in communities. It's a kind of poetry I can't teach; I can only learn from it.

Imagine *Speaking Back: Student Voices from Writing and Tutoring Across Cultures* as a space where young writers from diverse backgrounds study the tutoring of writing and then help one another create writing projects that contemplate linguistic justice, community engagement, and interdisciplinary inquiry. This is writing fortified by research, practice, passion, and feedback from trained tutors. Here are students with energy, grace, and powerful voices; they bravely write about communities, identities, and pedagogies. I am proud to introduce the work of writers making change and being changed both by their academic learning and by their community engagement.

Works Cited

Bailey, Steven K. "Tutor Handbooks: Heuristic Texts for Negotiating Difference in a Globalized World." Praxis, vol. 9, no. 2. 2012, http://www.praxisuwc.com/bailey-92. Accessed 18 Jul. 2022.

Blau, Susan, et al. "Guilt-Free Tutoring: Rethinking How We Tutor Non-Native-English-Speaking Students." *The Writing Center Journal*, vol. 23, no. 1, 2002, pp. 23–44. *JSTOR*, http://www.jstor.org/stable/43442160. Accessed 18 Jul. 2022.

Deans, Thomas. "English Studies and Public Service." *Writing and Community Engagement*. Bedford, 2010 pp. 97-116.

Edmundson, Mark, "In Defense of UVA. *Inside Higher Ed.* Nov. 27, 2017. https://www.insidehighered.com/views/2017/11/27/trials-and-triumphs-university-virginia-essay

Flower, Linda. "Writer-Based Prose: A Cognitive Basis for Problems in Writing." *College English*, vol. 41, no. 1, 1979, pp. 19–37. *JSTOR*, https://doi.org/10.2307/376357. Accessed 2 Aug. 2022.

Hanna, Monica. "'Reassembling the Fragments': Battling Historiographies,

Caribbean Discourse, and Nerd Genres in Junot Díaz's the Brief Wondrous Life of Oscar Wao." *Callaloo*, vol. 33, no. 2, 2010, pp. 498–520, muse.jhu.edu/article/385131. Accessed 20, July. 2022.

McCool, Matthew. *Writing around the World*. Continuum, 9 May 2009.

Mooney, Annabelle, and Betsy Evans. *Language, Society and Power: An Introduction*. Abingdon, Oxon; New York, NY, Routledge, 2019.

Nelson, Louis P. and Claudrena N. Harold. "Introduction: Dialogues on Race and Inequity at the University of Virginia." *Charlottesville 2017: The Legacy of Race and Iniquity*. Edited by Louis P. Nelson and Claudrena N. Harold, UVA Press. 2018, pp. 1-16.

Ratcliffe, Krista. "Rhetorical Listening: A Trope for Interpretive Invention and a 'Code of Cross-Cultural Conduct.'" *College Composition and Communication*, vol. 51, no. 2, 1999, pp. 195–224. *JSTOR*, https://doi.org/10.2307/359039. Accessed 20 Jul. 2022.

Sommers, Nancy, and Laura Saltz. "The Novice as Expert: Writing the Freshman Year." *College Composition and Communication*, vol. 56, no. 1, 2004, pp. 124–49. *JSTOR*, https://doi.org/10.2307/4140684. Accessed 18 Jul. 2022.

Williams, Sarah L. "The Peer Advisor Program." OAA virginia.edu. UVA, 11 July 2022 https://oaaa.virginia.edu/peer-advisor-program-1989-2009. Accessed 18 Jul 2022.

Vaidhyanathan, Siva. "Opinion | Why the Nazis Came to Charlottesville." *The New York Times*, 14 Aug. 2017, www.nytimes.com/2017/08/14/opinion/why-the-nazis-came-to-charlottesville.html. Accessed 16 Jul 2022.

Young, Vershawn Ashanti. "'Nah, We Straight': An Argument Against Code Switching." *JAC*, vol. 29, no. 1/2, 2009, pp. 49–76. *JSTOR*, http://www.jstor.org/stable/20866886. Accessed 26 Jan. 2024.

Part I: Into Communities

1 Fourteen Years' Difference

Mariam Mohamed

It's my first day as an English-as-a-Second-Language tutor. I'm excited, but I'm also as nervous as a freshman starting her first day of high school. I'm not really sure what to expect or how I will be as a tutor. Will I be able to explain things in a way the ESL students will understand? I am wearing a yellow shirt with jeans and black boots. I'm looking well put-together but feeling anxious deep down. I arrive at Upper Walker Elementary School and go to Ms. H's ESL classroom. I introduce myself: "Hi everyone, my name is Mariam Mohamed. I am a second-year student at the University of Virginia. I currently live in Northern Virginia but was born in Egypt." I look around the classroom and see two hijabi girls getting excited to see that I wear the hijab too. I smile and take a seat next to one of the hijabi students, named Aaima. She is using a school-issued laptop and borrows pencils and paper from the teacher. I can tell that her family is struggling financially. My smile fades, and I try to hold back tears as I remember how that struggle felt.

Fourteen years ago, I was Aaima. Fourteen years ago, my parents took my brothers and me on a journey to a place we never even knew existed—a journey from Cairo, Egypt to Brooklyn, New York. I remember being confused as to why we were there. Where were my cousins, aunts, and grandparents? Why was no one around me wearing the hijab, like my mom did—or speaking Arabic, the only language I knew? I remember that our new apartment was so small and that I hated it because our home in Egypt was so much better. I remember going shopping with my mom and only buying clothes that were on sale because we did not have enough money to buy clothes that actually looked good. Because one US dollar was roughly equivalent to sixteen Egyptian pounds, we barely had money. For the longest time, America felt like the worst place in which to live, and all I could think about was how I wished to be back in Egypt. We did not have money to buy basic school supplies, and I remember always having to borrow pencils from the teacher. Money was so limited that my mom would only buy things that were considered "necessary," which included things like groceries and clothes but excluded things like toys.

I remember that, during every lunch period, there was always the girls' table and the boys' table. While the boys were fighting with wrestling figures on skateboards, the girls were playing peacefully with these tiny pet figurines called the Littlest Pet Shops. Of course, I did not have one, so I was not allowed to sit and play with the girls.

One day after school, my mom and I went clothes shopping. I was getting bored of seeing her staring at clothes, so I wandered off to the toy section. Not surprisingly, I found Littlest Pet Shops, and they were being sold for $15 per animal figurine. I picked up the cute brown dog that had a pink bowtie and made my way to my mom. I was nervous to ask her if I could buy it, but I decided to take the risk anyway because I wanted to be like the other girls in school. I asked her, but, when I told her the price, she told me to "put it back—that is unnecessary."

Unnecessary? That piece of plastic that every girl has is unnecessary? Trying to buy something so I can fit in and have friends is unnecessary? I felt broken, saddened, and destroyed; I felt as if I was never going to be able to make friends. Here I was, this girl who didn't speak or understand English, who could barely afford anything—and I had no friends with whom to talk at school.

I see my childhood self in the students at Upper Walker Elementary School. After everyone settles down in Ms. H's classroom, she pairs up students and tutors. Since I am already sitting next to Aaima, Ms. H assigns me to work with her. She opens her school-issued laptop and goes to the reading website. She picks a random book and starts listening to the audio to get a good understanding of how the words are pronounced. After the audio is done, I decide to read it out loud to her so she can hear how the words are pronounced again. I ask her to read after I've finished, and she does just that. However, I start hearing sniffles between every other word. I am confused because just a few minutes ago she was fine. I ask her what's wrong, but she whispers under her breath, "Nothing." I am not really sure what to do other than just be physically there for her. I pass her a tissue and sit there next to her for a few minutes. I ask her if she wants to take a walk with me outside, and she agrees.

We leave the classroom and start making our way toward the playground. As we walk, all I can think about is whether to ask her what's wrong again. I do not want to seem like the pushy tutor/teacher who forces her to speak about something she doesn't feel comfortable sharing. Rather than making her talk about something that upsets her, I decide it would be better to just get her in a better mood.

I look at her and say, "Aaima! Tell me, where are you from?"

"I'm from Afghanistan."

"No way! I've never been to Afghanistan, but I heard the mountains there are beautiful."

She starts to talk about Afghanistan and its culture.

"Yeah," I say, "you know, I am from Egypt, and, over there, the kids always play soccer in the middle of the streets too."

We go back and forth about Afghanistan and Egypt, their similarities and differences, and how we miss our home countries. As she talks about something that brings her happiness, the conversation dries Aaima's tears. Not only do I want to show Aaima that we are similar in the sense that we are both immigrants, but I also want to show her that I am not much older than she is—and that she should view me as a friend rather than a tutor/teacher. I cannot think of any other way to do so than by sharing that I have a little brother around her age, and I start describing all the stuff that he does. We start talking about Roblox, an online game that is popular among middle schoolers; we talk about Youtube channels and all the "stupid" comebacks that sixth graders use. She starts laughing when I tell her about how my little brother annoys me and all the fights we have. Then she shares stories about her own siblings.

"My older brother is at school in Afghanistan. He did not come with us here because he has to finish school and take care of my grandma," she says.

"Do you miss him?"

"Yeah, but I call him on Facetime, and he shows me my grandma too."

After we do about three laps around the playground, Aaima seems to be in a good enough mood to go back to class and continue reading.

This walk that I had with Aaima probably meant more to me than it did to her. All I could think about was my older brother, Ahmed, when we first moved to New York. Although Ahmed and I started in the same elementary school, we had different experiences. I came when I was a kindergartner, but he was a second grader. Fortunately for me, my kindergarten class was neither mean nor nice; they just left me alone. However, Ahmed's second grade classmates were basically all bullies. For example, during the first month of school, Ahmed still did not have a backpack, so, one day, he and my mom went shopping for one. They went to Payless and saw a backpack with the character whom we now know as Dora the Explorer. Because barely any girls in Egypt have really, really short hair, both my mom and brother thought that Dora was a guy character.

He went to school with it the next day. Every day that week, my mom would get a call from the principal that Ahmed was crying and that they could not get the cause out of him. Eventually, my mom finally figured out that the reason was that many of his classmates were making fun not only of his backpack but also of his not being able to speak English. Ahmed said that they always said things to him that he did not understand and then laughed together about it. This almost seems like a scene from a movie, now, but it was the unfortunate reality that Ahmed had to face at that time. The bullying continued for months. Ahmed dealt with getting made fun of, being called names he didn't understand, and even getting his lunch stolen.

During my walk with Aaima, I could not help but think maybe she's sad because of the way someone is treating her. Maybe she is tired of being an outsider because of how she speaks English. Maybe she misses the comfortable lifestyle she was used to in Afghanistan. Or maybe she has personal problems happening at home that affect her directly. The cause of Aaima's and Ahmed's tears may or may not have been the same, but they are both immigrant students who have had to deal with the American public education system while barely knowing English. A lot of times, teachers underestimate how much immigrant students go through both at home and at school; they just expect them to give their all on school assignments. In a perfect world, a student would always put forth their best effort, but the reality is that immigrant students deal with a lot of personal problems, such as adapting to change, family problems, or bullies—and these challenges can distract them from learning.

I still remember when I had to go to school the day after our house got robbed. It was winter, and my mom, Ahmed, and I were coming back from grocery shopping. I was getting better at adapting to our new "home," even though it wasn't home to me. It was very cold, and I had on a really big, stuffed, pink jacket and a scarf my mom forced me to wear around my nose and mouth. I was holding my mom's hand. I remember that Ahmed and I were talking about how we really needed to go to the bathroom because we could barely hold it in. We finally saw the apartment, and I could not have been happier. As we got closer to the house, my mom's face tightened with fear and bewilderment. She stopped walking and stood in silence. I was confused and started throwing a fit, because I really needed to go to the bathroom. She told me that I needed to stop whining and that we could not enter the house because it was not safe. I was not sure what she meant by that, but I followed her lead as she turned in the other direction and started making phone calls. What I did not know at that time was that someone had broken our front window, gotten into the house, and stolen the TV—along with other items that my mom never told me about.

For a whole week, we had a big black trash bag taped over the broken window. I didn't sleep for fear that a random man was going to walk into the house and take more of our belongings—or, even worse, kill us. The feeling of fear was beyond what I can describe, and that killed me emotionally and mentally. Yet, every morning that week, I had to get out of bed and go to school as if everything was fine at home. I had to pretend that I did not live in fear and, instead, focus on learning English. I tried, but a lot of my teachers did not realize that I was not able to concentrate on classwork because my mind was busy wondering whether my parents were safe at home. I had no motivation to learn in school that week because I was just looking at the clock, waiting to see if my mom had survived to pick me up that day. This "home" was not safe.

Although I think it's safe to say that Charlottesville, Virginia is safer than Brooklyn, New York, a tutor cannot disregard the struggles of any of these ESL students because these struggles come in different forms. One of my ESL tutees, a student named Nour, has a lot of behavioral problems. Tutoring her comes with the challenge that you first must get past her attitude and convince her to sit and focus on her work. When I first met Nour, she always talked back to her teachers, didn't raise her hand, bothered other students, and walked out of the classroom. Usually, Ms. H. handled Nour's behavior with special care by staying as calm as possible and talking to her nicely, even if she was rude to her; however, one day, Nour had a verbal altercation with the PE teacher. He started yelling at Nour in front of her classmates and tutors and told her that she needed to lose the attitude. Obviously, Nour did not take that well, and she started to talk back. She was not willing to step away from the argument, and the two went back and forth, yelling at each other in front of everyone. Suddenly, Nour felt embarrassed that she was getting yelled at and put on the spot, and she started to cry, telling the PE teacher that he did not know what she was going through.

Although I agree that Nour needed to change her behavior towards teachers and classmates, I also felt sympathetic towards her; I know it can be very challenging being an immigrant and ESL student. As her classmates left PE, Nour refused to go because she was still angry and overwhelmed by emotions. I sat next to her, and she started talking about how the PE teacher was so mean to her. She said, "He is not my parent to yell at me like that."

I let her rant about him for a few more seconds and then asked what she meant when she told him he didn't know what she had been through. She opened up to me and shared that she was the oldest of six kids and that her mom had a lot of expectations for her; she had to help take care of her siblings, clean, and do homework. She explained that it was very hard and stressful because she did not have as much time as any other student to study or focus on assignments or reading for school. She added that, most of the time, she did not do her homework, which resulted in teachers getting mad at her. It almost felt like a repeating cycle of having a lot of responsibilities at home, not having time to do your homework, and then getting yelled at by the teacher. Now that I knew this about Nour, I was more careful about the ways I approached her during each tutoring session.

Because I have been impacted by personal problems at home, I am able to feel for Nour and just take it step-by-step with her, rather than giving her instructions all the time. For example, one day, I had to help Nour complete her multiplication packet. It was about six pages long, which Nour was already mad about, but I told her that, if she stayed on task, I would play basketball with her afterwards. She seemed happy about that idea, so we began right away. She did the first two pages with me, and then I started to see her losing interest and getting distracted by talking to other students.

"Come on, we want to make sure we have enough time to play basketball."

"But I have a blister, and I don't want to write."

I thought about this, and I came to the realization that I could be her writing hand, as long as she told me what to write, word for word. By dictating to me, she could focus on the material itself rather than on how much her hand hurt. We tried it—and we were able to finish the assignment in a timely manner, with no attitude or behavioral problems.

This is why it is important that teachers and tutors consider students' situations and search for ways to push them to do their best work without crossing boundaries. Pushing a student too much can cause them to become frustrated with the idea of learning something new, to hesitate to try new things, or even to hate a subject throughout their academic career.

I myself have been affected by teachers crossing my boundaries. When I was in the ESL program, I was always forced to read, read, read—even though there were a lot of days when I was upset at school because my parents back at home were financially stressed. I carried a lot on my plate for a kindergartner and felt responsible for my parents' actions. To this day, I feel that this financial stress and this demand that I adapt to a new environment made me mature quickly; I was forced to care about "grown-up" things rather than focusing my time on playing with toys like Littlest Pet Shop.

During my time as an ESL student, I felt that my ESL teacher did not care about me as a person, only as a student. Her only goal was to teach me how to write, speak, read, and understand English. I do not remember her once asking me about how life at home was or what Egypt was like. It was always, "Read this. Write this. Read it again." I hated ESL class with a passion. This feeling is not something a student is born with; rather, it grows, and ESL became the class in which I never got breaks, in which I had to read and write constantly. I remember that I would have days when I was feeling down, and my teacher simply gave me more books to read. Her routine was consistent: she read the book once to me, and then I read back to her. I was—understandably—a very, very slow reader, and she made me feel bad about it. Sometimes she would tell me I was doing a "good job," but other times I would have to "pick up the pace." I was trying my hardest to improve, but she was never pleased. It angered me at times; my time with my ESL tutor made me feel as if I couldn't pronounce most of the words on the page. I would never be able to read like a native speaker. It seemed unfair because I worked twice as hard as the other students in my grade, but they were reading books with ease, while I felt as if reading a few pages took me years.

As I got older and entered the second grade, my English vocabulary became richer. I was still in ESL, but a lot of my classes were with the regular, native speakers. I was still slower than other students, but I was getting better at reading faster. Yet, as time passed, my hatred for reading still grew, and there was another problem: not only did my teacher always tell me to pick up the pace, but she also wanted me to practice reading out loud to the class. While her pace-pushing had approached or even crossed my boundaries to some extent, she was now forcing me to do something way out of my comfort zone. I always felt embarrassed to read out loud to the class because I felt as if I was reading slowly and pronouncing some words incorrectly. To this day, I hate reading out loud because of the fear that I had when I was younger; I felt as if someone was going to make fun of the way I read. This is what I mean when I say that teachers and tutors should be careful when pushing students to improve or excel: too much intensity or too little sensitivity can lead students to develop long-lasting hatred for aspects of the learning experience.

Since I personally experienced being pushed too far out of my comfort zone when I was an ESL student, I am always very cautious with how I go about tutoring my students. For example, I also tutor a girl from El Salvador named Genesis. We did an exercise that involves reading a passage multiple times, and, because I hated when my ESL teacher refrained from giving me breaks, I made sure to give Genesis a break after reading a book twice. During our breaks, I either let her relax for two minutes or talk to me about anything she wants. I need to make sure that she can clear her mind before resuming her next task—or she risks developing a hateful relationship with reading. I also make sure to guide her through big words that are difficult to pronounce and reassure her that she's doing a good job when she attempts those big words. As an ESL tutor, I want Genesis to improve her speaking, writing, reading, and understanding of the English language, but I know that it is best if I don't put a time limit on this goal. In other words, every student learns at a different pace, and that is completely fine. Trying to rush a student to learn will never help that student reach her reading goals, so it is important to take time to let students relax and refresh so that they are ready to learn more.

Another thing that I am always cautious about when tutoring these ESL students is spelling. I refrain from telling them how to spell a word right away. I want my students to try to sound out the letters and write what they think the letters are before asking me how to spell a certain word. I do this because, when I was an ESL student, my teacher always helped me with spelling. I would barely have to try before she would tell me the correct way of spelling a word. Although I appreciated it then, that method of teaching did not help me in the long run because it never really taught me how to spell. To this day, I struggle to spell words, and I'm grateful for autocorrect.

Unlike the ESL tutoring I experienced as a student, my own tutoring practice centers on inclusion. When working with ESL students, one is always trying to answer the question: what will be the most efficient way of teaching these students? Some might think that one-on-one tutoring is best, while others might believe that ESL students should be placed in regular classrooms so that they can learn from their peers. However, I disagree with both of those approaches, preferring a middle ground. Having been both an ESL student and an ESL tutor myself, I believe that the best approach involves setting aside a class period during which ESL students can be together in a classroom. Students would still be able to be with native speakers in all their other classes, have dedicated time to practice English during their ESL class, and experience the community and support of a classroom full of other ESL students.

I believe that this is the most efficient and kindest approach because, growing up as an ESL student, I was taken out of recess to sit one-on-one with a teacher in a very small classroom. As a kindergartner, recess meant everything, and the fact that, instead, I had to do more schoolwork—while my classmates had fun playing in the sandbox—made me hate learning English. It seemed unfair to me that I had to do double the work and not have time to play. I remember the sadness that I felt every time I saw my ESL teacher come to pick me up during recess time. I wished I was fighting over which baby doll I would play with or who was going to be the mom and dad when playing family. I wished I was watching the boys run around playing tag or pretending to shoot each other. Instead, I had to stare at pieces of paper with pictures of objects that I now know as "car," "tree," "flower," and "house." It almost felt as if

I was being punished for not being able to speak English. I now know that was not the intention, but, for a five-year-old, the loss of recess felt like a form of punishment.

I appreciate that Upper Walker Elementary School does not exclude their ESL students. For ninety minutes a day, all the fifth and sixth grade ESL students are placed in the same class; although they are not getting the one-on-one help that I got, there are many tutors on staff to help individual students throughout class time. Being among peers may help each ESL student know that they are not alone in the journey to learn English. It shows them that they are not the only ones who recently moved to America and that it is okay to struggle because experience leads to growth and development. The students at Upper Walker Elementary School still spend time around native English speakers by attending collective classes throughout the day, but they get additional help by participating in an ESL class period and still have time to enjoy recess with their classmates. These students are putting in just as much effort as I did when I was an ESL student, but they get the sense of community—and the break—I never had.

Upper Walker Elementary School further includes their ESL students by highlighting the fact that they come from different backgrounds. Rather than making the ESL students feel embarrassed that they are still learning English because they were born and raised in other countries, the faculty always find ways to encourage ESL students to embrace their unique cultures and identities. For instance, the school puts on an "international day," when ESL students can present information about where they are from and what they love about their country/culture. The project itself is not only personal, and therefore fun for the students to work on, but also educational, because it gives them the opportunity to write paragraphs about aspects of their countries of origin—like cuisine, clothes, and history. It teaches them how to present to an audience and allows them to practice reading over and over again. Students may feel empowered by the experience of sharing knowledge they have mastered. The teacher cannot tell them what is right or wrong; instead, they are able to navigate freely through a topic they know better than anyone, to speak and write with authority in English. As I helped my students work on their projects, seeing them grow made me realize how important it is to take a step back from trying to teach ESL students about American society, and to ask them to teach us about their cultures instead.

Helping my students with these projects also made me wish I had the opportunity to do something similar when I was little. I think it would have helped me to build my self-confidence. I tried to hide my true identity—and, by "identity," I mean where I was from, what religion I practiced, and how I looked. Throughout my elementary school years, I tried to become as Americanized as possible. I remember refusing to take my mom's homemade Egyptian dishes to school for lunch because they looked and smelled "weird." Once, when I convinced myself that it was not a big deal for me to take my mom's food to school, a white girl named Elizabeth made fun of what I was eating. She sat there with her peanut butter and jelly sandwich while I sat there with my rice, lamb, and eggplant dish. I remember feeling so embarrassed when Elizabeth said, "Ew! What is that?" and proceeded to get up and move to the other table. From that day on, I refused all my mom's offers of Egyptian food and just ate bagels and cream cheese.

For a long time, I also had trouble acknowledging and expressing my true religion. I did not start wearing my hijab until sixth grade. Until then, I was basically denying that I was Muslim; there was no physical sign of my beliefs. Growing up in America after 9/11 made it really difficult to want to claim my religion. Although I knew that Islam was not the reason why 9/11 happened and that that event can only be blamed on terrorists and not a religion, saying I was Muslim had a negative connotation that I hated. Little Mariam did not want to be labeled as a terrorist, so I tried my hardest to cover up my Muslim identity. I remember being required to bring a parent to book fairs, someone who could pay for the things we wanted—and I never wanted my mom to come with me because she wore the hijab, which would blow my cover. Instead, I begged for my dad to come because he looked like a regular, middle-aged guy with no specific religion attached to him. To little Mariam, admitting to being Muslim was like asking to be bullied because I thought the world hated us.

I also tried to hide my natural features. For example, I went to a predominantly white school, and many of the students around me had straight hair. As a child, I always had very puffy, thick hair. I hated it so much because I did not think it was pretty. I remember telling my mom to straighten my hair every other day because I felt that I could not go to school with my hair all puffy like a ball. Because I was comparing myself to the white students who spoke perfect English and seemed not to have struggles outside of school, I was insecure about many of my physical features.

Since neither my teachers nor my school showed interest in unique, diverse backgrounds, I felt as if my cultural identity was not worth sharing, as if no one wanted to know about who I truly was; for that reason, I wanted to push away my identity. I wanted to be like the majority—like every white student—so that I could fit in and not be seen as this immigrant student who had "weird" hair, "weird" food, and who associated herself with a "terrorist" religion.

That's why I want to emphasize the importance of asking about and being interested in ESL students' backgrounds. As a former ESL student, I can promise you that we do not find it rude if you ask us questions about our culture or religion; it actually makes us feel important, in the sense that we get to talk about our own cultural experiences, acknowledging and celebrating how they might differ from someone else's cultural background.

Back in Brooklyn, there was an ESL final examination at the end of each year to see whether or not a student was ready to leave the program and be out on their own. It was my least favorite day—full of anxiety, stress, and fear of failure. And I did fail; I failed the ESL test my first and second years. Longing to get my recess time back and not be excluded anymore, I wanted nothing more than to pass that exam.

After several years in the ESL program, and hating it day after day, I finally passed the exam. I remember waking up an hour earlier than usual to get a good breakfast, turning on the TV, watching the Disney Channel (to get me excited for my least favorite day!), and praying a little extra to God to help me pass my ESL exam. I really did not want to fail again. I remember that, as I was getting dressed, my stomach started to hurt because I was so anxious. I walked to school in silence alongside my mom; the exam was the only thing on my mind. The bell rang for recess, and all my classmates were happy and joyful, but I dreaded what was to come. The usual routine commenced, and my ESL teacher came and took me to that depressing room with white walls and no pictures. I sat on the squeaky chair with a packet and a freshly sharpened pencil in front of me. Before I picked up the pencil, I said a quick prayer, begging God one last time to help me pass. I wrote my name on the first page and then started my exam. The first question had a picture of an *arybia*.

First question: "What is this a picture of?"

I knew it. It was an *arybia* in Arabic, but what was it in English? In that moment, I could not remember, so I went to the next question.

Second question: "The car drove past the big tree. Which one shows a picture of a tree?"

Easy. Tree is *shagrah*. I circled the tree with no hesitation. Then I re-read that statement and realized that the *arybia* mentioned in the question before was the car. I felt as if I had just solved a Rubik's Cube. I went back to the first question and wrote "car" for the answer. The first two questions gave me hope that, maybe, I did have a chance at passing, and I began to feel more confident. When I finished the exam, I got up, handed it to my teacher, and went back to the classroom, my steps buoyed by just a dash of optimism.

A couple days passed before I got pulled out of the classroom by my ESL teacher. I was confused; the recess bell had not yet rung.

"Am I in trouble?"

She did a short, fake laugh and said, "No, silly. You passed your ESL exam!"

I was above cloud nine. I tuned out everything that came out of her mouth after that and felt a smile big enough to show all my teeth spread across my face. I was free, or at least thought I was.

What I failed to see the day I passed my ESL exam was that, although the school system did not consider me an ESL student anymore, I would never master English, never reach the level of a native speaker. Fourteen years later, I still see myself putting in double the effort to get the same grade as a native speaker. It may not look like it because I work hard, but I still struggle with reading, writing, and speaking in English. The funny thing about being a multilingual student is that, in America, because there are a lot of words I don't understand or even know how to say, my English feels below average. But, when I go back home to Egypt, everyone I know thinks my English is the most perfect English one could speak. The reality is that I will always be an ESL student, even when I am an ESL tutor, because learning English is a never-ending process.

As that journey continues, I plan on using what I have learned through my experiences as both an ESL student and an ESL tutor to become the most effective speech pathologist I can be. In my opinion, being a speech pathologist is very similar to being a tutor because my client and I will practice speaking phrases, reading books, and communicating more generally. I will be taking my own advice by giving clients breaks, not pushing them beyond certain boundaries, and being mindful of personal issues that they may be facing. Essentially, my clients will be like ESL students, and I will be the speech pathologist/ESL tutor.

As in the case of ESL tutoring, one of the most important priorities for a speech pathologist is building that tutor-tutee friendship. I really want to take the friendship I never had with my ESL teacher and turn it into a positive bond between my clients and me. I will be using similar strategies as the ones I use to form friendships with my ESL students, including asking them about their background, trying to relate to them, and finding unique ways to make each session fun rather than dreadful. I will help clients be able to communicate effectively; I am speaking back to the world about my miseducation through the practice of speech pathology.

2 Learning from Refugees

Ahmed Mohamed

Abstract

This piece is an academic discussion of tutoring practices as they pertain to refugee learners. Through a discussion of rhetorical listening and the translingual approach, I reflect upon and challenge relevant scholarship through the lens of my personal experiences tutoring refugee students in Charlottesville, Virginia. The piece makes the case that the Writing Center Studies discourse community should seek to implement and maintain approaches that welcome and advance the writing of multilingual refugee students. It is important to be inclusive of this growing discourse community.

Introduction

Charlottesville, famously a college town at heart, is less known for its bustling, growing refugee community. However, the academic outreach initiatives set up by the International Rescue Committee allowed me to connect with this discourse community. For the past two years, as a student at the University of Virginia, I've been tutoring two adolescent refugee students, Musa and Ahmad—an experience I have found to be not only rewarding, in the sense that I'm able to give back to my community, but also enriching, because tutoring challenges me to grow as a learner. Even though both my tutees and I speak fluent Arabic, tutoring presented many communication challenges. I'm writing this piece both to communicate my experiences and to suggest improvements to common approaches to tutoring the refugee community.

Tutoring refugee students often involves working with multilingual learners who are working to develop their use of the English language. As a result, refugee students rely heavily on their native tongues to communicate ideas, express concerns, and convey understanding. I expected to hear and speak Arabic during my tutoring sessions, but I was unaware of the difficulties that would come along with my students' use of Arabic. Most of my students were Syrian, Iraqi, or Jordanian; each spoke a different dialect of Arabic. This would be my first introduction to the many Arabics that exist within the refugee community. For my entire life, I have relied on my strong fluency in Egyptian Arabic and my elementary understanding of Saudi Arabian standard Arabic, called Fusha. I had expected to lean on this knowledge base when tutoring my refugee students, but, when I tried to express myself in those dialects, I was met with confusion and awkward silence.

I sat down with Musa, a freshman in high school, to discuss a personal narrative essay he had just been assigned. I asked him what he would like to write about, and he replied with a very general but intriguing answer: "My journey." I nodded and smiled in excitement, but, as the conversation continued, I realized that I was falling behind in understanding some of the ideas he was trying to communicate. I consistently found myself interrupting Musa mid-sentence to ask for clarification. For the first time, I was encountering the difficulty of understanding Musa's Syrian dialect, with its unfamiliar vowels and distinct pronunciations. His different vocabulary made his sentences seem choppy, and I was trying to decipher one sentence while attempting to listen to the next. Eventually, I lost track of his message. When I asked for a clarification, he attempted to explain but did so in his Syrian dialect, which did not help much. It was a mutual effort, as Musa tried, for his part, to piece together the bits of my Egyptian Arabic that were familiar to him. Interestingly enough, Musa and the rest of the refugee students often understood my Egyptian dialect because Egyptian movies, shows, and songs dominate Arab popular culture. I usually got the gist of Musa's ideas, but I sometimes called on Ahmad, another refugee student who was more familiar with the Egyptian dialect, to help translate what Musa was saying. I didn't like to involve a third person in the conversation between a tutor and tutee, but it was a quick and sometimes necessary solution. This story highlights the importance of listening; it's a challenging but essential skill for tutors to develop.

There are several pieces of scholarship that provide useful insight into working with multicultural learners and tutoring refugee students. Carol Severino's "Crossing Cultures with International ESL Writers" highlights the role tutors play as cultural informants: we introduce international students to the nature of American writing traditions within the context of American history and culture. Severino discusses her own experiences tutoring international students and her understanding of why international students often make certain "errors" in writing—moves that would be considered mistakes by English instructors. More generally, Melissa Ianetta and Lauren Fitzgerald's *The Oxford Guide for Writing Tutors* lays out a plethora of practices that can make for a successful tutoring experience. In particular, the second section of that book, "A Tutor's Handbook," reminds tutors to be patient, observant, and understanding of students. It also provides techniques by which a tutor can cater to a student's interests, establish trust, and set educated goals.

These practices rely on the tutor's ability to listen, which Krista Ratcliffe discusses at length in "Rhetorical Listening: A Trope for Interpretive Invention and a Code of Cross-Cultural Conduct." Recognizing that, in writing center praxis, tutors often focus on the text rather than on the writer, Ratcliffe advocates for the use of rhetorical listening as a part of a larger effort to understand the individual needs of tutees. Likewise, in "Language Difference in Writing: Toward a Translingual Approach," Bruce Horner, Min-Zhan Lu, Jacqueline Jones Royster, and John Trimbur also push for the implementation of a newer approach. As a means of challenging the language used in academic settings, these authors draw a distinction between "standard" English and "edited American English." In academic papers, writers are often thought of as using "standard" English, but Horner et al. would argue that "standard" English contains many dialects and operates in a variety of spheres—and that academic writing is actually "edited American English." Tasha Laman and Katie Van Sluys's "Being and Becoming: Multilingual Writers' Practices" ties together some of these tutoring strategies by providing educators with a framework for establishing a classroom environment that is enriching for both multilingual learners and their English-dominant peers.

While current literature emphasizes the need to be open-minded and highlights the importance of tutors creating "zones where different cultures meet, often cultures with language barriers" (Wolff 44), little has been written about what happens when speakers use very different dialects. Horner et al., who push against the conception of the standard version of a language because they believe that the decisions a writer makes regarding language use reflect their social experiences in the real world, might advocate for different dialects of Arabic intermingling. They view such differences as creative outlets for purposeful self-expression rather than as barriers.

Rhetorical Listening

As mentioned briefly above, rhetorical listening enriches the learning experience of both the tutor and the tutee. In her article "Rhetorical Listening: A Trope for Interpretive Invention and a Code of Cross-Cultural Conduct," Krista Ratcliffe discusses how significant this practice is in the tutoring process. To her, rhetorical listening "signifies a stance of openness that a person may choose to assume in relation to any person, text, or culture" (217). It's important to note that Ratcliffe's notion of listening goes beyond just giving one's attention to a sound; it mandates that the listener ask about an individual's identity, how their experiences shape their work, and how they are shaped by their cultures and histories. By improving the quality of the conversation, rhetorical listening allows tutors to understand their tutees on a level that goes beyond the tutoring session. For this type of listening to take place, however, the tutor and tutee must occupy a shared environment that allows both sides to be open to all types of written, oral, or imaginative discourse.

As the title of her article indicates, Ratcliffe describes rhetorical listening as an inventive process. Ratcliffe writes:

> rhetorical listening turns hearing (a reception process) into invention (a production process), thus complicating the reception/production opposition to invite rhetorical listening into the time-honored tradition of rhetorical invention. Second, rhetorical listening turns the realm of hearing into a larger space, one encompassing all discursive forms, not just oral ones (220).

In the context of tutoring refugee students, Ratcliffe's first and second "turns" suggest that the tutor must not only pay attention to the tutee's comments, but also assess and act upon features of a conversation that are often overlooked. When Musa described the topic of his personal essay as being his "kisa," or journey, I needed to be mindful that the word "kisa" implies a long, time-consuming collection of both arduous and pleasant experiences. To transform hearing into a production process, I needed to consider his status as a refugee and build upon that in our conversation. This kind of sensitivity allows for the building of a positive rapport and provides guidance as the student's paper finds its direction. Most importantly, it establishes an open environment in which the student can comfortably discuss their concerns about their assignments. This comfort is especially significant for refugee students, who may carry trauma from their home countries, find it challenging to discuss certain paper topics, struggle to relate to their schoolwork, or feel uninterested in completing assignments. Rhetorical listening empowers the student by providing them with an opportunity to identify with their work and to view their writing as a means of self-actualization. The tutor is also enlightened in the sense that they become conscious of the difficult experiences endured by their refugee tutees. It's a humanizing acknowledgment that allows tutors to be empathetic with their tutees as vulnerable, yet strong, beings.

Ratcliffe's third turn, the idea that rhetorical listening places the responsibility of intent on the listener, indicates another skill that tutors must develop to best serve the academic needs of their tutees. She states, "third, rhetorical listening turns intent back on the listener, focusing on listening with intent, not for it" (220). By urging the tutor to "focus on listening with intent, not for it," Ratcliffe pushes tutors to view the tutoring process as one of communication building rather than of grammatical revision. In tutoring refugee students, it's critical for the tutor to listen intently to the tutee before guiding them through the revision process. For example, when first discussing Ahmad's book analysis essay, I made the mistake of engaging with the text by making a series of recommendations that had always helped my own analysis-focused English essays in high school. I found Ahmad nodding in agreement but failing to engage in an active conversation about my suggestions. Realizing this disconnect, I decided to take a step back and ask for his initial thoughts on the paper's organizational layout. It was only after listening with intent that I understood Ahmad's reasons for wanting to stick to his original plan for the paper. I had mapped my own experiences onto his paper, expressing my insights at the wrong moment and creating an environment that did not nurture rhetorical listening.

In her fourth and fifth turns, Ratcliffe communicates the idea that rhetorical listening contextualizes a text as part of a larger cultural setting while still satisfying the goals of the tutor and tutee. She writes:

> Fourth, rhetorical listening turns the meaning of the text into something larger than itself, certainly larger than the intent of the speaker/writer, in that rhetorical listening locates a text as part of larger cultural logics. And

fifth, rhetorical listening turns rhetoric's traditional focus on the desires of speaker/writer into a harmonics and/or dissonance of the desires of both the speaker/writer and the listener. (220)

In working with Musa on his personal essay, I found that he was not developing his story as I would have expected. Instead of building on each part of the story, Musa's essay amounted to a mere an iteration of facts and events. I later learned that this was the norm for Middle Eastern Arabic writing. It was clear to me at the time that he was not yet familiar with the conventions of academic writing and the culture of English teaching and learning in the United States. Before introducing such conventions to him, I had a discussion with Musa about how he wanted to convey his "journey." Working within the context of the American academic standards through the Observation, Evidence, Analysis (OEA) paragraph structure, Musa was able to develop and articulate his ideas with much more depth. By maintaining a balance between the tutor's suggestions and the tutee's receptivity, a tutoring session can become a productive, healthy learning environment in which all participants are able to understand each other as people.

While I was able to listen rhetorically to Musa throughout our sessions, my reliance on Ahmad for translation purposes sometimes made our exchanges feel stilted and unnatural. Having a third party mediating the conversation complicates the task of rhetorical listening. Everything that reaches the tutor is an edited reiteration of the tutee's original speech. This is problematic in the sense that what the middle party chooses and, more importantly, chooses *not* to relay can have a significant impact on what is being conveyed; aspects of the tutee's comments can get lost in translation. As a result, it becomes especially important for the tutor to listen for their tutee's intent— as a means of extracting the most out of what's being relayed by the third party. This focus would go against Ratcliffe's recommendation of listening *with* intent. When a third party is involved, the tutor must focus on understanding the assignment and how the tutee wants to write it. Because the translator may experience conversational fatigue or even struggle to grasp the ideas they are relaying, it becomes much more challenging for the tutor to ask refined questions about how the tutee is approaching their work.

I experienced this difficulty when Musa was asking about writing his hook. Ahmad mistook Musa's explanation of his approach as referring to his thesis statement, rather than to his hook—a misunderstanding of which I became aware only after noticing Musa's confusion as I spoke about thesis statements. I was fortunate to have tutees who understood my Egyptian dialect of Arabic because, had I not, the conversational repair would have been much harder to initiate. In situations where the tutor and tutee do not understand each other's dialects, a third party is necessary, and this complication of Ratcliffe's bi-directional exchange makes it even more important for both sides to listen for one another's intent. While this dynamic ultimately reduces the effectiveness of rhetorical listening, it is a necessary accommodation for effective tutoring in the refugee discourse community.

Translingual Approach

Multilingual refugee students deserve a tutoring approach that values linguistic diversity. Musa and Ahmad, who are both Syrian, are from different regions of Syria and therefore speak different dialects of Syrian Arabic. Musa, who hails from the Western coast of Syria, speaks the Sahil (coastal) dialect, distinguished by the heavy use of the letter 'Qaf.' Ahmad, who is from Damascus, speaks the Shami (Damascene) dialect, which is popular on Syrian television and known for sounding softer and having more stretched vowel sounds. These are only two of the four spoken dialects in Syria. Arabic is very rich in linguistic diversity, which makes it a challenge for Arabic-speaking outsiders to fully understand one another if they're not familiar with the specific dialect that person is using. While challenging, this diversity poses an opportunity for learners to gain new knowledge about variations within a language—and within the culture of its speakers. Likewise, these variations among dialects, which tinker with the meanings and connotations of words and phrases, reciprocally shape the worldviews of their speakers.

Translingualism, as discussed in "Language Difference in Writing: Toward a Translingual Approach," celebrates this diversity and teaches language users to "assume and expect that each new instance of language use brings the need and opportunity to develop new ways of using language, and to draw on a range of language resources" (Horner et al. 312). As the world becomes more interconnected, translingualism makes it possible for learners to attain familiarity while working across language differences in writing. The translingual approach is the practical application of translingualism and advocates for changes in how language competence is defined. Specifically, the translingual approach seeks to empower language users to mold language to specific ends, acknowledges the linguistic diversity of language users worldwide, and challenges the English monolingualism status quo. The spirit of the translingual approach inheres in the conviction that the nature of language is "heterogenous, fluid, and negotiable" (Horner et al. 305). My refugee students showcase this characteristic of language by speaking and embodying a wide array of world Arabics. Their transition into American classrooms should be met not with pressure to conform to monolingual English norms but with curiosity about their oral and written language use. By viewing their linguistic differences as resources, teachers can organically empower refugee students to voice their perspectives. Refugee students are often forced to flee their home countries, leaving behind the discourse communities that have served as significant parts of their identities. As a result, educators should strive to welcome these identities with open arms and create platforms for self-expression.

The translingual approach upholds certain standards in writing, ensuring that refugee students are still gaining the linguistic skills necessary for successful, competent self-expression. Educators implementing this approach do not dismiss outright the notion of errors in writing; they exhibit open-mindedness about what they would normally deem a mistake. Challenging the norm of what's considered quality writing creates an avenue by which language can be performative. As an Arabic speaker writing in English, I sometimes find myself wanting to include a word in Arabic that best captures the essence of an idea—but I don't do it because it would go against the conventions of a standard academic English paper. It would be both practical and liberating to use my linguistic background to attempt a more sophisticated, representative expression of my ideas. In this same sense, refugee students should be able to use the rhetorical conventions of their native languages and code-mesh within their academic writing. With the option to implement such an approach, Musa's personal narrative essay might have communicated a deeper, richer perspective.

The translingual approach not only encourages organic writing but also allows the reader to participate in an active learning process. In this active process, the reader encounters new rhetorical styles and must engage with the writing to understand it. Furthermore, this dynamic allows the reader to think beyond the traditional monolingual English with which they have operated throughout their education. This experience launches a process of self-reflection by which, since they likely use a different rhetorical style of English in their personal life than in academic writing, the reader may cease to see themself as monolingual. Additionally, active engagement with a translingual text enables the reader to better understand the writer—what they represent, how their experiences have shaped their writing. The reader realizes that they have something in common with the writer: a shared translingual use of language. By building this bridge, readers can better empathize with refugee writers. This empathy is especially important since the refugee crisis is at an all-time high, exacerbated by the increasing levels of anti-refugee rhetoric and misinformation in the United States. The translingual approach gives refugee students the agency they need to combat such discrimination.

While translingualism pushes for the exploration of and openness to diverse linguistic styles among all parts of society, I would add that translingualism should also be the standard in dealing with all other languages (not just English) and in supporting multicultural students coming into a composition classroom. My experience with Musa and Ahmad showcases the richness that exists within the Arabic language alone, indicating that the use of "standard" Fusha in Arabic writing classes limits the expression of many other dialects that would otherwise honor the diversity of the Arabic language and the linguistic heterogeneity of its users globally. The reader of Arabic academic texts might never be offered exposure to these global Arabics. The implementation of translingualism in Arabic academic writing has the potential to educate Arabic speakers around the world about one another.

Teaching One Another

Tasha Laman and Katie Van Sluys's "Being and Becoming: Multilingual Writers' Practices" provides educators valuable insight into establishing a fruitful, enriching classroom environment both for multilingual students and for their English-dominant peers. By creating writing exercises that provided multilingual students with the freedom to write in their native languages, Laman and Van Sluys invited their students to examine the connections and differences among their comprehension of their first language(s) and of those they were learning. Even the English-dominant students started to compare English with other languages as students "shared their linguistic knowledge with peers as they leaned into one another's notebooks during writing time, read their writing aloud during share time, and publicly displayed their writing during celebrations" (273). While Laman and Van Sluys suggest that a diverse classroom maximizes the richness of such exchanges, my experiences working with Musa and Ahmad show that there can be diversity and learning even when learners share what is essentially the same language. This is the direct result of the diversity that exists within every language and a reflection of translingualism's value that even a monolinguistic speaker can technically be multilingual.

Conclusion

From their various world Arabics to distinct personal journeys, drawing upon their personal journeys and varying languages and dialects, refugee students provide educators and tutors with a glimpse into the richness of linguistic resources that multilingual students bring to their writing. As individuals resettling into an often vastly different country, they oftentimes lack the agency to produce organic writing in their new discourse communities. As a result, they are pressured to quickly adjust and conform to the monolingual English standards of academic writing—and are at risk of losing parts of their linguistic identities. To mitigate this risk, educators and tutors must rhetorically listen to their students, implement a translingual approach to writing, and adopt cross-cultural writing exercises. While these are all steps toward better understanding and celebrating refugee learners, these approaches may not work in all contexts, so tutors must also find creative ways to best meet the needs of their multilingual students. Since every tutor and tutee each bring different sets of experiences to the tutoring session, they might encounter some obstacles impeding clear communication, understanding, and transparency. However, these obstacles ultimately serve as opportunities to learn from one another.

Works Cited

Horner, Bruce, et al. "Language Difference in Writing: Toward a Translingual Approach." *College English*, vol. 73, no. 3, 2011, pp. 303–21. *JSTOR*, http://www.jstor.org/stable/25790477. Accessed 1 Jan. 2024.

Ianetta, Melissa, and Lauren Fitzgerald. *The Oxford Guide for Writing Tutor: Practice and Research*. Oxford University Press, 2016.

Laman, Tasha Tropp, and Katie Van Sluys. "Being and Becoming: Multilingual Writers' Practices." *Language Arts*, vol. 85, no. 4, 2008, pp. 265–274, www.jstor.org/stable/41962279. Accessed 23 Sept. 2023.

Ratcliffe, Krista. "Rhetorical Listening: A Trope for Interpretive Invention and a 'Code of Cross-Cultural Conduct.'" *College Composition and Communication*, vol. 51, no. 2, Dec. 1999, pp. 195–224. *JSTOR*, https://doi.org/10.2307/359039. Accessed 3 May. 2020.

Wolff, J.M. "Tutoring in the Contact Zone.'" *Stories from the Center: Connecting Narrative and Theory in the Writing Center*, by Lynn Briggs and Meg Woolbrigh, Urbana, IL, National Council of Teachers of English, 2000, pp. 43–50.

3 Fading Dreams: A Retrospective on American Education

Thaqeb Chowdhury

Abstract

This paper examines my experiences as a second-generation immigrant weighing desires against expectations. In it, I reflect on the traditional education pathway set for the modern-day student and how I personally navigated the challenges it presented. The experiences laid out in this piece demonstrate how powerful outside factors are in shaping us, in some cases asking us to strip away our personal interests in favor of success. The paper recognizes that there are ways to reignite passion for learning new talents outside of the traditional school system and advocates for such experiences to be made available to students as their curiosity blossoms.

As I stepped off the school bus with my first sixth grade report card in hand, I remember having a distinct feeling of pride. To tiny eleven-year-old me, sixth grade was the toughest academic challenge yet. Assignments had become more arduous, time felt more precious, and old school friends were beginning to drift away. Despite these pressures, I was able to keep up with most of my classes—but not English. English was the area in which I suffered the most. Every prompt focused on subjects and grammar rules about which I just didn't care. None of this interested me, and my low first quarter grade reflected that.

Nevertheless, the rest of my grades were stellar in my eyes, so the moment I stepped foot in my house, I excitedly shoved my report card into my mother's hands, expecting nothing but praise for all my hard work. As my mother intently scanned the paper, her brow furrowed. My beaming smile slowly disappeared, and I braced myself for impending judgment.

"Why is the English grade so low? If you tried harder, you easily could have done better," she said disapprovingly in her Bengali accent.

Confused by her reaction, I responded, "But didn't you see all my other classes? I did pretty good overall! And I tried really hard this semester. English is just so boring; there are too many rules to remember!"

She rebuked me with a lesson that has since been etched into my brain: "There are no excuses for this. You can't get ahead in life by being 'pretty good.' You must be the best in school, or you'll be left behind, just like your dad and I."

As harsh as her statement felt to my younger self, I knew that she spoke from a place of good intention. Both of my parents immigrated from Bangladesh to the States just a year before I was born. Even though the two of them had lived as comfortably as anyone could in a third world country, they gave up everything to ensure that their future children could experience a proper education and acquire well-paying jobs. However, as with many difficult decisions, their actions had a cost: coming to America meant becoming members of the lower economic class. What my mother told me all those years ago was an echo of her sacrifice, a plea for me to work as hard as I could academically so I could someday support her and the rest of my family.

While my family didn't suffer from extreme poverty, it was clear to me growing up that my parents were living paycheck to paycheck and barely scraping by. Both of my parents held bachelor's degrees from well-known Bangladeshi colleges, but—as with many immigrants from third world countries—these degrees might as well have been scrap paper in America. They have both bounced between low-paying jobs ever since coming to this country seeking income wherever they could find it. I echo my father's wise adage about the college search: finding employment these days is less about what you know and more about where you learned it. From their own experiences, my parents knew that an education from a well-respected institution in the "right" field meant the difference between a life of struggle and a financially stable future. My parents urged me to do well in school to secure a better life for the whole family.

After that conversation with my mother ten years ago, I adopted her words as part of my identity, always pushing myself to be the "best" in all my courses and never settling for anything less. Classes stopped feeling like places for learning; instead, they became steppingstones to the next evaluation. Proving myself by excelling in my coursework meant everything to me, so testing and projects became the unhealthy focus of my life. School was no longer about serving my curiosity; it was about paving a path to financial success and repaying the sacrifices that my parents made for me, ensuring that they did not make the difficult decision to come to this country in vain. As noble as the cause felt, I can admit that these pressures weighed on me heavily as I worked hard to maintain my grades.

Now, as I near the end of my academic career for the foreseeable future, I've begun to realize just how much my mother's words about education rang true. In my experience with the American education system—as I worked tirelessly to appease my parents' hopes for me—I've realized how cold and unforgiving it can be. In my view, the closer one gets to the upper echelons of the education system, the less it feels like a system oriented toward learning. Instead, there is increasing pressure to limit one's failures and to prove oneself on the first try, rather than demonstrating marked improvement and building mastery over time. The American education system's focus seems largely focused on preparing students for the next step in their careers, molding students into ideal candidates for recruitment. Pursuit of interests outside traditionally "respected" fields is a luxury afforded by time and money, one that many low-income students like me simply cannot risk taking due to the expectations placed upon them.

With this piece, I aim to illustrate my grievances with the current educational system and its cultural impact through my own personal experiences. My familial and economic circumstances urged me to conform—though begrudgingly—to the education system, resulting in the many frustrations and lessons upon which I will reflect in this piece. While I recognize there is no easy solution to the conflict between profitability and passion that the education system, and perhaps society, perpetuates, I hope that my retrospective can help others understand the frustrations that underprivileged students face in academic settings.

Looking back, I regret abandoning my dream career path because of academic and familial pressures. During my high school years, I had dreams of becoming a journalist, which is somewhat ironic considering my early struggles with English. In ninth grade, I took a news writing class on a whim—and to fulfill an elective course requirement. I initially thought of the course as nothing more than a grade booster, a simple course where I could relax while adapting to the difficulties of high school coursework. However, with every class I attended and with every lesson I learned about what it meant to be a journalist, news media began to pique my interest more and more.

The teacher of the course, Mr. Wojcik, a former journalist and author, remains one of my favorite teachers because of how much he contributed to developing my younger self's journalistic dreams. He had all the characteristics of a stereotypical writer: a slender man in his late 20s, bearing stylish, full-rimmed frames and a signature soul patch. His manner of speaking was always composed and engaged; his teaching style was calm, opening his classroom as a place of learning rather than of evaluation. Mr. Wojcik was one of the few teachers I had who seemed genuinely to care about his class's subject material, and he wanted to pass on his passion for news writing to his students.

Most of Mr. Wojcik's classes went against the conventions to which I was so accustomed in regular school life. For one, he didn't believe in traditional evaluations. He knew that for many of his young students, myself included, this was their first exposure to news writing, and they needed time to develop their skills. Instead, he elected to make most of his course participation-based to encourage us to explore and expand on techniques we learned in class. Every few weeks, he would call on us to write a news article on any topic that intrigued us, asking only that we try to implement what we learned over the past few sessions into our piece. If we demonstrated effort and interest in the subject material, we would receive the full participation grade. In response to our work, he would provide us detailed notes of his thoughts on our papers, providing positive feedback and constructive criticism wherever he saw fit.

I was utterly confused about how to even begin the first assignment from Mr. Wojcik. With previous schoolwork, following rubrics and guidelines to the letter was all I needed to do to get a good grade, and, with the pressures placed on me by my parents, that was what mattered to me. None of that applied to these assignments. While, in retrospect, I see that this change should have relieved me, it ended up causing me more stress.

I struggled during our first writing session, and I resolved to confront Mr. Wojcik about the assignment after class. After I voiced my frustrations and asked him if there was anything specific he wanted to see in my future work, he responded with a slight chuckle, finding the young, flustered student in front of him quite amusing.

"You don't always have to appease someone else, Thaqeb," he explained. "In my class, I want you to focus on yourself and what you care about, here and now."

At first, I didn't fully grasp what he was getting at, but, as I slowly pieced together his views on education over the course of many conversations, I began to understand. Growing up, Mr. Wojcik always resented school because it never felt like he had a chance to express his own interest in his classes; instead, he did what was necessary to get the grade and move on to the next class or institution of learning. To him, coursework didn't feel like they were designed to better our current selves; instead, they focused on continuously preparing us for the next career milestone. While he accepted that evaluations were necessary to judge one's progress in a field, to him they seemed to take precedence over actual education, with classes focusing heavily on preparing students for rote testing. Metrics for future college and job recruiters meant everything, and students' own interests and ability to apply what they learned to the real world had become increasingly sidelined.

Outside of the occasional art or creative writing class, there was no outlet for Mr. Wojcik, no way to tell others what he really thought about the world. It wasn't until he graduated college that he felt free to make his own decisions, choosing to become a writer to impart his opinions and observations to others. Although he knew that being a writer likely wouldn't reap the sort of salary many of his peers were earning in other fields, he went ahead with the profession because it embodied choice and expression, providing an escape from the expectations of society imposed through the education system. Mr. Wojcik came from an affluent family, and his parents promised to support him as he pursued his dreams and help him during the more difficult times.

He eventually became a teacher because he knew many other students probably felt the way he did when he was younger; they were trapped in an academic system focused on efficiency over everything else—a system that simply wanted to create the next homogenous generation of skilled workers, forgoing creativity and mental stimulation in favor of rote evaluation methods like arbitrary grading scales and standardized testing. Everything was in service of the next step: you performed well in high school so you could get into a good college; then, in college, you repeated the same thing in pursuit of a decent living. In Mr. Wojcik's eyes, schoolkids didn't have a chance to live in the present and explore their current passions because they were always being forced to meet expectations and become cogs in the workforce machine. Over time, I began to share many of his frustrations with the education system, particularly as college grew nearer and my parents' pressures grew heavier.

To combat the norms of the education system, Mr. Wojcik designed all his English electives around freeform assignments that weren't traditionally graded. He believed that by taking away the pressure of strict evaluation, he could make it possible for students to think beyond the classroom and bring real world knowledge to the table; he wanted to allow them the sort of freedoms that he had craved during his own years in school. Despite his seemingly lax grading policy, he made sure to provide detailed feedback with every assignment. He aimed to see growth in his students' writing ability over time and believed that providing personalized feedback would help them in this regard.

As I attended more and more of his classes, I came to appreciate Mr. Wojcik's outlook on education. I respected him greatly for his encouraging demeanor towards students and his genuine interest in teaching writing. His enthusiasm for news writing in particular was something I came to share, and I believed that I could eventually realize my dream of becoming a journalist. I adored the idea of writing about events as they unfolded around us, as if I was some sort of recordkeeper who would inform generations to come. Editorial pieces were my favorite pieces to write, as they let me share my opinions about global and local happenings. Above all, I continued taking Mr. Wojcik's journalism classes every year of high school because they gave me a break from the burdens of graded judgment in other classes, and because they afforded rare opportunities to feel like an individual in school, rather than another competitive, overachieving student desperate to boost his class rank. His assignments gave me an outlet to be myself, untethered from the pressures of my parents and peers.

Unfortunately, Mr. Wojcik's class was an exception from the norm. The more time I spent in his class, the more I began to realize this truth. The systems in place were designed for simplicity and efficiency, created specifically to pressure students to focus on certain areas of study rather than to explore their interests. The GPA is one of the more egregious examples of these systems, as it was designed to standardize and simplify a student's academic prowess, representing many of my teacher's and my own frustrations with our education system.

The GPA is a flawed attempt to measure a student's proficiency by condensing grades across their academic career into a single number. It is absurd to think that one's performance in dozens of distinct classes across many fields of study can be distilled into a single number. Yet, for some reason, a high GPA requirement has become the de facto gatekeeper for many opportunities, leading many students, me included, to focus on improving this number over actually cultivating our own interests through education.

In fact, the GPA goes so far as to actively discourage improvement and academic exploration over time. Initial failures are immortalized in the GPA; it averages grades across all classes, without giving any additional weight to meaningful improvement in a field. While improvement in subsequent classes can be seen on something more detailed like a transcript, the GPA typically acts as the first selection criteria in determining which applicants are deserving of a closer glance. As a result, many students are discouraged from taking risks they deem fruitless, potentially losing out on more varied academic paths. For these reasons, the GPA feeds into the ideas that education is simply a tool to move ahead in life and that the pursuit of other interests is a luxury that only a privileged few can enjoy.

Throughout my entire time in high school and college, it felt as if the GPA was an essential part of my identity. As college grew nearer, my parents would constantly pressure me about how high my GPA was. Almost every conversation about college or the future would lead back to my GPA, with my parents often mentioning a comparative standard they wanted me to meet, like the average GPA of students who got into some prestigious university or the GPA of the child of a family friend. Their concerns surfaced incessantly, and, even now, as I stand on the cusp of graduation, they continue to pester me about it. The metric was their simplified way of measuring whether I was on track to the successful life they desired for me, and they were determined to make sure I attained their lofty expectations.

As I entered college, fears of falling short of the high GPA requirements for future job applications drove me away from my dreams of becoming a journalist. While I knew there were plenty of classes available to help me expand on my news writing proficiency, I worried that harsh grading criteria and the heavy workload of these classes could possibly damage my GPA, making me an unappealing candidate to employers. My economics major was as difficult as any English or media studies major, but the potential reward of a well-paying job in that field, in my mind, easily outweighed the GPA risk. With expectations to economically support my family constantly looming over my head, it was clear that I had to shelve my goals of being a journalist to focus on my major.

While I wish I could say I eventually followed in Mr. Wojcik's footsteps and pursued my passions, there was too much on the line—in terms of my family obligations and salary prospects—for me to become a journalist. The difference between my teacher and me is that he came from a well-off, established, American family, so, if he fell somewhere along the way in pursuit of his dreams, he had a support system that would pick him right back up. For me, there was no safety net; if I failed, I would be taking my family with me into the depths of the lower class. School was my only chance to break the cycle of poverty, so I couldn't afford to take risks.

While I don't necessarily regret becoming an Economics major—I eventually came to enjoy all the fascinating complexities of that discipline—I'm saddened by how much of my original interest in journalism has been lost. While I initially tried to pursue news writing courses and organizations at UVA, I ultimately chose to abandon them to focus on Economics to boost my potential as a favorable job candidate. Again, everything was oriented toward the next step in life; for someone with my obligations, there wasn't much room for unconventional personal interests.

The American education system's hyper-focus on preparing generations to become ideal candidates for the workforce leaves little room for students to explore fields like art and English, fields that don't provide the same financial yield as STEM and business disciplines do. For children from low-income families, typically members of minority groups like me, these pressures to follow convention are only amplified, as education becomes the only real pathway to success.

So, the question then becomes this: can we solve these issues within the education system? Based on experience, I can't say I have faith that we can. Formal education and economic opportunity have been fundamentally intertwined in our society. In addition, with time and money on the line, many of these educational institutions choose to value admission requirements such as standardized testing and quantifiable metrics like the GPA over students' demonstrations of their developing proficiencies through personal, passion-driven projects. Although it may be difficult to change the conventions of the formal education system, I've seen that private and personalized tutoring can act as an excellent educational alternative, providing an outlet for children to exercise creative freedom without the pressures of formal schooling.

In my final semester of college, I served as a volunteer for Computers for Kids (C4K). C4K is a non-profit tutoring organization that provides underprivileged children with necessary resources and a safe, welcoming environment in which to explore their creative potential. When I first began tutoring here, I was blown away by the advanced technology and artistic materials made available to these kids. All throughout C4K's brightly colored building were examples of the amazing things these children had made with the guidance of experienced tutors. On display were complex robotics, artistic masterpieces, and all other sorts of creative accomplishments that I wouldn't have even dared to attempt as a child.

Although access to resources facilitated the children's interesting creations, it was the tutors who made the real difference. They helped the children mold their budding ideas into fully formed projects. What differentiated these tutors from teachers in a traditional school was that they weren't tethered to the obligations of grading and testing. There were no standards to meet and no future obligations to strive towards in that space; instead, there was boundless freedom to help tutees showcase their unique traits and interests. Personal tutoring, when done right, isn't about helping students achieve high marks; rather, its goal is to help students advance their personal skills and grow as people.

My favorite personal experience as a C4K tutor involved a young girl—I will call her Brianna—who asked for my help in experimenting with photography. I saw a lot of myself reflected in Brianna. She too came from a lower-class family and felt the expectation to excel in school and help lift her family out of poverty. At C4K, though, those pressures didn't weigh on her. There was no one to formally evaluate her work and leave feedback that would follow her for the rest of her academic career. With such freedom, she chose to use her time there to develop her photography skills.

Back when I still had dreams of being a journalist, one of the topics we covered in Mr. Wojcik's journalism classes was photography, and we learned that every good story is supplemented by eye-catching but informative visuals. My previous experience with photography was a tremendous help for Brianna as I helped her navigate camera settings and apply some of the techniques that professional photographers use. Over our tutoring sessions, we experimented with different subjects as we worked to create the most interesting photos possible. During this encounter, learning wasn't a one-way street the way it would be in a traditional school setting; we both taught each other what we knew about photography as I helped her explore her creative interests. In the end, our tutoring session was cut short when her parents came to pick her up early. However, in the time that I spent tutoring her, I felt as if I was transported right back to my high school self, vicariously living out my own dreams as I helped Brianna realize hers.

It's these sorts of personalized experiences that, in my view, the formal American education system lacks. Rarely do schoolchildren get the opportunity to explore new fields and develop their interests without the consequences of evaluation weighing on them. For underprivileged kids, these pressures are only exacerbated by the fact that school has a direct link to job prospects, forcing students like me to avoid riskier, but more personally engaging, educational paths. Personalized tutoring sessions focused on helping students rather than evaluating them can showcase education's capacity to reach beyond preparation for major life milestones. Helping children grow their interests in the present, rather than advance their interest in the future, should be a priority of all education, and I believe that many educational institutions would do well to follow C4K's lead in implementing more low-pressure assignments–especially for low-income students who feel constrained by the current system.

4 The Way Through the Nostrils: An Attempt to Remember

Caitlin Gerrard
钟凯琳

Abstract

In his article "The Classroom and the Wider Culture: Identity as a Key to Learning English Composition," Fan Shen compares American transcendentalism and Chinese "yijing," uncovering the profound differences between Western and Eastern rhetorical styles. Eastern rhetoric does not rely as heavily on logic or argumentation as Western. Instead, Eastern rhetoric finds its power in aesthetics. This experimental memoir examines an American student's bicultural background by inscribing their memories in the Chinese style of "yijing." The piece reveals how explorations into the writing styles of other cultures can help bicultural writers reconcile their clashing cultural identities.

> *There were the same luxurious smoothness of surface, the same scarcely perceptible tendency to the aquiline, the same harmoniously curved nostrils speaking the free spirit.* — Edgar Allen Poe, "Ligeia"

Rarely do I find the emptiness in which to spontaneously think. In free space, I would like my thoughts to happen *self-so-ing*. Like nature, like 自然, at once Western and Eastern. In English, nature is twofold. It is the broadest substance of the physical world and the most inherent substance of each person and thing. In Chinese, nature, or 自然 (zìrán), is what is so of its own. 自 can be read as "nose," and 然 can be read as "so." In unison, 自然 is our perception of things *self-so-ing*, just as they naturally are. In this experiment, I wish for my nature to exist as 自然, for my English substance to be sculpted out in a Chinese way that leaves it as uncarved and as real as possible.

Walking home, a smell startles me awake. An odor, slightly metallic and slightly noxious, aerates my memory and flies me back to a city far away.

Momentarily, I leave Charlottesville, slipping underneath the cement to my 叔叔's apartment in Shanghai. Flavors of cigarette and smog intermingle, bringing me back to the red laminated floors and the turtle-spotted ponds, the Chinese summer school and the 生煎包.

While the aroma of smoldering tobacco is familiar in Charlottesville, these scents seldom move me such vast distances. This scent was unique, particularly Shanghainese. I do not detect it anywhere else. My last visit was eight years ago, yet my nose remembers it without hesitation.

The stench comforted me, arriving as a waft of familiarity in an unexpected place. My nostrils became the entrance for realization; the current entered my body, the foreign particles passing through the organs and the brain, bringing along with the air a thought:

Where am I walking, so contentedly?

I am not actually very Chinese. Europeanness seems to dominate most of me. My name reads across: Caitlin Gerrard. My sister is Jane, my father is John, and my mother is 月. Laid out in a line of words, the language of my life tips towards the same imbalance.

For most of my childhood, my family and I lived together in Virginia, in a two-dimensional-looking red house with a blue roof and a huge Japanese maple tree sprawling out in the front yard. In the backyard, my dad had planted several little trees to conjure an appearance of wilderness. Along the fence, my mom interrupted his wilderness with her garden of vegetables. These vegetables were ferocious; her large Chinese zucchinis climbed over fences, crushing up to the tops of neighbors' trees where they would hang and swell. My mom had raised these zucchinis to be like herself. They encountered boundaries, they went beyond them, and they loudly prevailed.

Inside our house, you could see the business of life. Masses of shoes smearing the floor, dress shoes atop riding boots atop waterproof slippers. A pantry curiously infinite, occupied by boxes of pasta and bottles of 蚝油. In the basement, three cellos: one old, one young, one in the middle. Standing in the dining room, a rocking horse named Misty. Levels of books, ranging from the scrawly ink of *The BFG* to the disintegrating sentences of *The Sound and The Fury*. Beneath the couch, tufts of Australian Shepherd fluff. A piano, a keyboard; an acoustic guitar, an electric guitar. The house is a picture of our different occasions—our excesses and our pressures, our developments, and our accidents.

My sister and I were raised in this house, in this free space in between. Like most creatures, we originated in the productivity of our parents. In this family, we each have an origin: my dad began in Rahway, New Jersey, my mom began in Shanghai, and my sister and I began in Northern Virginia. Collectively we stretch across, connecting and covering a generous surface area.

I am hesitant to describe my parents. As a person (re)produced, my relation to them seems the most infinite relation I will ever have. I feel I have seen their roundness, making them impossible to disclose in two-dimensional type. Furthermore, there is much about their lives that remains unknown to me. All of this discredits the authenticity of any description I could provide. Therefore, I will resort to describing them optically, as they might appear to someone they have just encountered.

My dad has a respectful presence. He is a little awkward, but in a hospitable way. He is pretty tall and slender, and his walk is a little wonky since his hip is made of metal. His mind tilts toward the thoughtful and neurotic. His interests are spread out: he enjoys camping, cooking French cuisine, watching *Seinfeld,* practicing Hapkido, running, and reading *Lord of the Rings.*

My mom's presence is more clamorous. Her voice travels quickly and loudly; each footstep pounds with a purpose. Her laugh, in particular, is thunderous. She is compact and a little clumsy, and she speaks to people unabashedly. Mentally, she is tough. Her spirit is in music—she came to America on a cello scholarship, and she has taught cello since before I was born.

Between these two people, something burst, and I, Caitlin, erupted outwards in all my human length. I am a little scatterbrained and very sentimental. I retain my dad's contemplation and my mom's volume. I love the color green, the guitar, rhymes, and *BoJack Horseman.* All these words connected to me appear freestanding on the page and in the imagination. Yet, if followed through for long enough, each one delicately winds its way back to its original authors: John and 月.

I was a bit of a nuisance as a child. Jane was pleasant, and I was provocative, rebelling whenever the world did not proceed according to my preferences. My tantrums were extraordinary; I could scream for hours straight. As a retaliatory tactic, my mom fell back on linguistic camouflage. I think I exhausted her so completely that she had no fragment of energy left to exert towards a more unfamiliar language. Her emotions outran her English, and my mom would passionately project towards me in 汉字. Amid each tumultuous reaction, my mom assigned me a name obscure in meaning: 跟屁虫 (*gēnpìchóng*). Later, I would discover the English equivalent: "fart-bug."

During my elementary years, my friends and I would tinker in the creek, the cold current circulating through our amphibious toes as our minds filled with observations. I saw the details: the quick cluster of tadpoles, the toothed repetition of leaves, the singing dribble of water. Nature was complex, was generous and exuberant. In all its multiplying forms, I found that I was part of the greater abundance.

Inside the white walls of the cafeteria room, I was temporarily disconnected from the abundance. "What is that fishy smell," my companion grimaced, her face mutating in disapproval. "Fried rice," I replied. I was confused. I smelled nothing strange. Fried rice was barely an exotic food. At home, my mom was slurping down fish eyeballs. However, at the lunch table, smells registered differently. I learned that, to some, the aroma of foreignness was intolerable. Her comment did not necessarily alter my spirit. It seemed more like a new sensory data point.

During recess, odor controversies continued. The autumn wind had brought with it a new playground villain: the brown marmorated stinkbug. I felt partial to the stinkbug—I still do. I do not understand what it is about them that so appalls. I found a keen enjoyment in looking at them. They appeared valiant, whittled into little heraldic shapes. The stinkbug was, to me, a perfect creature, utterly gentle and utterly misunderstood. To my classmates, the stinkbug was an enemy, flying place to place and exhaling its smelly chemicals all over the playground.

But who was I to walk away from the miasma? This was my heroic age.

"It smells like rotten ravioli!" one student snickered. "Why don't we squish it?" another suggested. My ears rang with those wicked words. It stirred my blood, and I sped forth, weaving amongst them to sweep up the victim in my grasp. I ran towards the wilderness, moving towards the slim possibility of safety. While running, I glanced down at my hands. Oozing out of its thorax, a glistening, transparent liquid flowed along the valleys of my palm. I felt a little betrayed, but I persisted. I entered the habit of saving stinkbugs, earning me the playground title "The Stinkbug Worshipper."

跟屁虫, "fart-bug." My mother's instinct was correct. There is in fact a sort of harmony discoverable between me and the 跟屁虫. An "invasive species," the original stinkbug arrived on my playground from China. How does it all fall together? A shocking smell, a disruptive child, a linguistic collapse. Is the world so nimble in its carelessness? Nature has a place for the 跟屁虫 as well as for me. Forms of pollution, of migration, prophesy a shared nature among everything and everyone everywhere. But why is it that some of us are still considered deficient?

There are some things that will never become familiar. Writing may reveal a faint and shadowy knowledge of a forgotten unity, but I will never see and smell it in its vividness.

Arriving in the United States, my mom had no guide. An unaccompanied traveler, newness surrounded her. I imagine it was confusing, living in a world with a mind so different from your own. Everything I think, I think in my native language; it coalesces effortlessly with the language of my environment. For my mom, the methods of her interior world mismatched with the methods of her actual world. It was continual opposition, inside and outside. This unfamiliarity will never become familiar to me.

What is familiar is suspension amid opposition. My parents had a somewhat volatile relationship. I wish I could be less pessimistic about the possibility of cultural integration. However, my childhood observations made it seem very futile. I saw the door bolted shut, heard the taut creak of the floorboards, felt the hostility whispering through the vents. Everything was complicated by the resoluteness of our family's geographic placement. We live in the United States. My dad would always be correct. He was to some extent only *seeming* correct, but, within the finitude of walls and words, he was correct. It was unfair, but it was true. I have never broken away from American space. Yet my American house still makes those celestial circles.

During adolescence, the steam began to open my eyes. Caucasian vapor—I breathed it out, and I breathed it back in. I became hypersensitive to Chinese moments. They made me wince. The culture became a chore. Although I spoke Chinese first, my memory of it was irretrievable. At school, at my desk, I inscribed my past onto the material of homework and tests, studying the cadences of a former self…but it was mandated. These mispronunciations and stumbles: they were not of me. The pencil prick wrote each stroke on its own. I was numb towards it. My mom would speak Chinese, and I would become sullen as soon as the sound hit my ear. But the remaining half of me could not stand upright alone.

In high school, I would always misplace my lunchbox. Underneath the desk, on top of the cabinet, in the corner of the cello locker—my little lunch pouch could dwell in so many places. Persistently, I failed to remember. It deeply frightened my mom. It probably was one of the things for which I was reprimanded most. She strayed from the typical Asian parent stereotypes, the typical 虎妈. Discussions of my grades were casual and often congratulatory. Discussions of my lost lunchbox were full engagements, lasting until we were both empty. She would increase the intensity and the volume, maintaining that I could not survive on my own if my thoughtlessness continued. I did not understand why it was so urgent to her. My dad, also, did not think it was so critical. It was not something I could help. My memory was irretrievable.

Like many high school students, I felt untethered. I was like my lunchbox, landing as if at random in the everyday locations to which I was directed. School seemed like a dreary simulation—waking up, driving, perambulating within the building, driving, studying, eating, sleeping. I walked round and round in a ring of paralysis. I considered myself no one, nowhere, doing nothing. But nothing is only nothing in relation to something.

Sometimes that something would loom up inside of my head. It happened so suddenly, I could float apart into stipples, into panic, into a perfume that dissolved me in the air above and above. The bricks would start to shudder. The floor would begin to wobble. Suspiration and hesitation. I could break the cycle. I could discontinue. A sigh and a stop. Surely, the whole collapse was happening. High above, each atom belonging to me learned to cling, hanging on heavily and helplessly until finally trembling back down to my blood-driven body.

Only half myself, I lost my footing. Sometimes I panicked in my room, sometimes in the library basement, sometimes in the bathroom stall. In these enclosures, I lost equanimity, but I found something in words. Forming feeling to syllable, I could shape myself in new letters, the sounds aching across the edge of each page, pulling unruliness forward in sheets of clear geometry. Out there, in language, I might be read.

I might be folded back up into a legible form. I might be perched back on top of a desk and understood.

妈妈，我继续睡觉。

Entering college, I followed what I had known myself to feel. I enrolled in English classes, and I enjoyed them. My excessive emotionality had found its academic place. I also enrolled in Chinese in order to fulfill an academic requirement.

In English, I began an enthusiastic education, moving swiftly from Dickinson to Morrison to Shakespeare to Dickinson again. Tight turns, steep slopes, occasional inversions—the words and the spaces sent my imagination into locomotion. The daunting task of writing surprised me with a new satisfaction, a satisfaction that started within, fell out through my fingertips, and then carried fulfillment back into my brain. The work did not fatigue; creative energy resurfaced as muscular activity. When I thought I did something really great, I could begin revolving. Is anything I write even that good? Probably not. I have been writing attentively for two years. Every time I glance backward, I am humbled a little more. Nevertheless, that feeling of satisfaction sustained me. A new freedom. I could give it all away and allow those letters to fill the page, to fill myself.

It has mostly been this way: me disappearing into English. In essays, in discussions, I spent each day generating small meanings. My awareness could be productively pushed away. My professors taught me to write with an architectural mind, to abide by a prototype plan and a prototype structure. Eloquence would decorate the edifice. One point would fall into the next, all compiling into an argument uniform and tall. I learned to write convincingly. I learned, I think, to write in a way so sophisticated that my ideas could intimidate. While it supplied an excitement, I could occasionally sense a certain something forced in its culmination.

At night, that certain something returned to me. The same something that struck me in high school, it returned during my second semester of college, but now with more threatening vocabulary. The quietude of my midnight dorm room unbolted the entrance for unfriendly thoughts. I could never achieve silence—the reverberation of my eyelash brushing the pillowcase could startle me into panic, propelling me awake until the early hours of the next day. I existed beside myself in undying observation. The wind under the door, the hurried contraction and dilation, the clatter and chatter from within. The panic would not subside, persuading the remnants to panic in accordance. Silence was no longer a peaceful absence. It was an invasion of everything, and in excruciating quantities. Language had turned its back on me, sustaining the sounds of my dismantling.

It is tempting to release oneself into wordiness, but prolixity folds back on itself with a sleep-eating suspense. Although I am devoted to English, I feel I have already sounded its oppositions. I wish to say that there is nothing uncomplicated about language, but I also wish to say that language is the most uncomplicated impulse. Therein lies the original issue. These sentences may appear unbending along the axis, but everything rotates around in circles.

During my second semester of college, all students returned home. It was a time I think everyone remembers too vividly. A thunderclap of germs and an awkward distance between bodies. The most there was to do was to lie alone and wait until you heard something express itself in the walls. My family was still tense, so I spent much of my time attempting to collect myself outside. Against the background of a viral apocalypse, I tried to save myself by listening to someone else.

In those April days, every morning was the same but different. Between my dad's maple trees, I would sit until I was moved by something in my surroundings. A coffee mug in hands, my pupil expanded on the velvety morning light, particle-waves striking the skin of my leg and splaying out in waltzing shadows. The reflection bounced off the babyish leaves, batting a green hue my way. Sometimes, I found it beautiful. Sometimes, I found it horrifying.

Writing everything out, it is difficult for me to locate distinct memories from this period. It has faded. Every day was the same—I remember the series now as a blurred and weak repetition. It all evolves into something too bleak. A queasy time; I will not prolong the chapter…

I now live in a place of more concrete dimensions, an apartment complex arranged in gray and hollow squares. Although these interiors are less leafy, life feels more natural in this scheduled setting. There always seems to be something to be remembered, something set on solid ground.

Fridays are treasured days. I awaken expectant, equally dazed and determined. I heave myself up from a mattress-curved sleep, eat a bowl of oatmeal and sip my coffee, sit for a moment with my hamster, and promptly head out, locking the door behind me. In the mornings, I enjoy walking. I must walk with huge steps; I have Chinese class at 9AM. For fifty minutes, my mind chases the logograms—

在中文课，我们先做小考试，叫听写．然后，我们的老师教我们新汉字和语法．虽然中文课比较难，我觉得我喜欢上．我四个学期认识我的同学们，我们都是好朋友，让我很高兴．下课以后，我回家．

Once back in my apartment, I idle with my roommates, sometimes watching cartoons or playing guitar before I depart for the library. Twisting my keys in the ignition, I begin the drive. My speakers make their infinite rumble, and "Blue Skies" splits the air as the whole stratosphere travels right there above me. The library is such a pleasant place. It is enthusiastically colored; walls of yellow, green, and blue intersect. I take the elevator to the third floor and join Linda in the classroom. Students trickle in, chuckling and chitchatting. From Bhutan, from the Dominican Republic, from India, everyone arrives together. It is a room of jovial words. All students are custodians of the same school system, and they have been learning English together for years. Everyone except Carlos, who started this semester.

Because Carlos is a new student, Linda cannot instruct him and the rest of the class in unison. He has no English proficiency and therefore requires individualized instruction. During most classes, Carlos and I sit at the other end of the room, drilling sentence structures and memorizing vocabulary.

"Me, mucho loco," Carlos giggles, pointing at himself. Together, we have been working for a couple minutes on enunciating the word "valley." The *vuh* sound is bent slightly out of shape. Carlos instinctively replaces the *vuh* with a *buh* or *duh* sound, as it is sounded in Spanish. The English *vuh* is always escaping, as if hidden in some low area, running between the hills of his alphabet. We continue our back and forth—"valley," "balley," "vuh," "duh," "vuh," "duh." Sometimes, the syllables do not find their way out of the crevices, but Carlos still moves forward. He is an intent learner, and he does not allow these little obstacles to stump him.

With literacy, words are nearly transparent, clarifying as soon as the eye lands. For Carlos, every word must be deciphered. Road signs, hospital forms, workplace conversation—he must listen and look with extreme awareness. His anguish is private, an anguish that cannot be communicated so simply. Because I have never had to endure it directly, I feel that I should not speak on it too extensively.

"To make a cake, you mix a little sugar, a couple eggs, and some flour," Linda describes. "Flower?" Xuefei asks. Linda perks up, realizing the source of the confusion and moving towards the board. On the board, she writes *flower* and *flour*, one above the other. "This is a flower," she states, holding up a pink Carnation flower she had brought into class. "Flour is a powder for cooking—Caitlin, would you come up and write your name on the board?" I get up from my chair and write across the letters: *C-a-i-t-l-i-n*. "Great," Linda says, writing *K-a-t-e-l-y-n* below it. "Caitlin and my granddaughter have the same name, but they are spelled differently," Linda says. Altogether, we pronounce "Caitlin" sound-by-sound, starting with *Cai*, like "cake," confronting a sly *t*, ending with an expected and effortless *lin*. "There are endless ways to spell it, people keep on inventing more," Linda explains.

There are so many Caitlins. So much has remained, in other forms, unspoken. A person so dependent on words, I cannot speak to 凱琳 fully. It is a thick truth. Hard to articulate, even in this overly familiar voice.

You hold each word for a moment in the ears and eyes. The sight, pictured by heavy and light opacities. The sound, rounding and flattening through the surface. Everything I know is bound by contrasts, which is maybe how I could know myself.

I could know myself through the oppositions between John and 月, between me and 我. Each side only standing by leaning on the other. Two forces, interdependent, create themselves. The 阴 (yīn) and the 阳 (yáng): the sunlight hits certain spots of the shaded valley, portions of dark and light playing with each other. What is obscured and what is obscuring, the light and dark always alternating. Two teardrops swirl together into a circle divided, one side always within the other.

Holding this circle in my hands, I release it, allowing it to roll on its way. It goes where it will, guided by the 道.

This thinking causes me to think more.

Why is it that my words discriminate among the senses? My thoughts accumulate slowly on this eternal blankness, each letter existing as the preeminence of sight and sound—what creates it and what it creates. Scent remains far more awkward to articulate. Maybe a touch of something filters through a story, the faintest trace of a molecule. I do not think it can all be visual and auditory. There must be something I can remember through my nose.

So, what is that smell I am missing?

On my way to class, I notice a familiar face at the crosswalk. A woman who looks like my mom stands next to me. I smile at her, and she, understandably, glances at me with mild confusion. Usually, this reminder would not sting so much. However, at the present time, I am not sure how much longer my mom will be in this American space.

Over Thanksgiving, I discovered that my mom must move back to China. She landed herself in an unfortunate situation. There, she will be in a better place. It was not something that anyone in my family had fathomed—for her, especially, this unanticipated movement has been startling. I have been realizing this future detail by detail. The thoughts expand: I think about the distance and the time, and the jarring conflation of both. I think about why I had to originate at such cruel distance from the person that I originated from.

我的妈妈是我, 但是她离我很远.

Things are beginning to appear differently. Some formation of sadness hangs over, gray and cloudy. It dims my senses, but, for her and for me, I try to remember:

sadness can be stimulating. It is a contrary truth, but I should still remember it. Even to call it a thought would be inadequate. The contradiction is a memory, a memory stored in my mind as a truth proven by the past.

The contradiction rises into a soothing giant. This hallucination, as welcoming and as large as a home—it holds me, and it rocks me.

Every landscape is composed of the same land. The only difference is the details. My eyes, my ears, and my nose settle the ground. My mom, although far away, will still be walking this same landscape. Together, in our standing places, we will make those same planetary motions. In this projection of space, I walk every day with a known direction. But there is an alternative direction, one subtly smelled. An imaginative magnetism, negative and positive—将来的道路应该是这样走的.

Works Cited

Poe, Edgar Allan, and Perry, Bliss (ed). *Fall of the House of Usher: Ligeia*. Doubleday & McClure co, 1897.

Shen, Fan. "The Classroom and the Wider Culture: Identity as a Key to Learning English Composition." *College Composition and Communication*, vol. 40, no. 4, 1989, pp. 459–466, https://doi.org/10.2307/358245.

Part II: Across Disciplines and Through a Pandemic

5 What Writing Center Studies Can Learn from Gender-Affirmative Psychotherapy

Anonymous

Abstract

Writing tutors and psychotherapists often work with clients who exhibit non-normative behaviors. Multilingual writers do not always conform to standard English conventions. Likewise, transgender and gender-expansive individuals stray from norms of gender expression. Both gender-affirming psychotherapists and scholars of Writing Center Studies have grappled with the question of how best to support these nonconforming individuals, but neither group has drawn from the scholarship of the other to identify potential solutions. This paper shows that both disciplines use similar social learning models to understand how individuals acquire language skills and gender identities. I argue that gender-affirmative psychotherapy provides a framework that writing center tutors can use to affirm the identities of multilingual writers and to help them produce "standard" English writing in order to accomplish professional or personal goals. I also assert that, like gender-affirming psychotherapists, writing center tutors can teach multilingual writers to view conventional English writing as a means to an end, rather than as a reflection of their true self.

> "The despotism of custom is everywhere the standing hindrance to human advancement."
> —John Stuart Mills, *On Liberty*

Introduction

No one knows for certain how human beings acquire two of the most fundamental components of social life: language and gender. Scholars have long sought to answer questions about the origins of human language. Nearly a century ago, modern scientists began to focus on questions related to the formation of gender identity. An increasingly accepted truism related to both categories is that culture significantly informs the way they function; dominant forms of speaking, writing, and gendered behavior differ across cultures and time periods. Societies ascribe prestige to certain performances of language and gender. We are rewarded or punished depending on how well we reproduce such patterns. Within the past forty years, scholars and activists have begun to criticize widely held beliefs about how "normal," and, by association, how "correct," these patterns are.

Those who write about working with multilingual writers now tend to celebrate this group's ability to use English in diverse and creative ways (Horner et al.). Similarly, many clinical psychologists assert that transgender and gender-expansive identities should be embraced. And yet, scholars have not yet articulated the link between gender-affirmative clinical standards and best practices for tutoring multilingual writers. In this essay, I attempt to bridge the gap between Writing Center Studies and gender-affirmative clinical psychology. I contend that conceptualizing writing as similar to gender is useful because doing so can help us understand styles of multilingual writing, and it can lead us to new strategies for working with multilingual writers. I begin by comparing theories of language acquisition and theories of gender identity acquisition that are currently held by scholars of Writing Center Studies and clinical psychology, respectively. I then describe similarities between approaches to working with multilingual writers and approaches to working with gender-expansive individuals. Finally, I argue that writing center tutors can adopt gender-affirmative practices to better serve writers who are learning how to write in English. My aim is to offer conceptual and practical tools for working with writers who may enter environments where "Standard American English" is highly valued, while also fully affirming that it is important to subvert the notion of one "standard" English.

Terminology

I will begin by briefly defining some terminology related to gender. A person's *sex*, the anatomical features related to their reproductive system, is distinct from their *gender*. Gender relates to the social organization of people into different categories, the most common of which are boy, girl, man, and woman. Some people, however, resist this categorization and identify as non-binary. Gender is thought to be *socially constructed*, meaning that different behaviors and roles (what we call *social norms*) are associated with different gender categories (World Health Organization "Gender and Health"). Typically, a doctor *assigns* a binary sex (male or female) to a child at birth depending on the appearance of their genitalia. Similarly, those around the child typically assign them a binary gender (boy or girl) corresponding to their sex assigned at birth. Sometimes a child's *gender identity*—their internal sense of being a boy, girl, or non-binary person—or their *gender expression*—the way they communicate their sense of being a boy, girl, or non-binary person to others—does not align with their assigned gender. In this case, the child can be described as *gender-expansive*, though previously these individuals were labeled *gender-nonconforming*. *Transgender* is also often used as an umbrella term to describe people whose *affirmed* gender, the gender that they identify with, differs from their assigned gender.

A Brief History of the Gender Affirmative Model

Between 1980 and 2013, the *Diagnostic and Statistical Manual of Mental Disorders* (*DSM*)—a publication of the American Psychiatric Association that mental health professionals use to diagnose mental disorders—included the diagnosis "Gender Identity Disorder." The criteria included the "strongly and persistently stated desire" to be the gender not associated with their sex assigned at birth, as well as verbal insistence that they were the gender not associated with their sex assigned at birth (Zucker et. al, 478). When working with children who exhibited this kind of behavior, therapists used behavior modification techniques to make boys more masculine and girls more feminine. The most notorious example is George Rekers, who in the 1970s developed a method that required parents to give effeminate boys a blue token every time he did something they deemed masculine, and a red token every time he did something they deemed feminine. Rekers instructed the father to "spank" the child once for every red token he collected at the end of the day (Rekers 173). He and other influential psychologists justified the intervention by asserting that gender-expansive children would be bullied by their peers if the gender-nonconforming behavior was not corrected.

Activism and clinical research focused on transgender and gender-expansive individuals throughout the early twenty-first century prompted the authors of the *Diagnostic and Statistical Manual* (DSM) to remove the diagnosis and replace it with the less pathologizing category of "Gender Dysphoria" in 2013. The American Psychological Association and the American Academy of Pediatrics published guidelines of care, in 2015 and 2018 respectively, that asserted that gender diversity is natural, and that a child should have the "opportunity to live in the gender that feels most real or comfortable to that child and to express that gender with freedom from restriction, aspersion, or rejection" (Hidalgo et al. 286). This approach is called the Gender Affirmative Model, and it has rapidly gained traction in the United States within the past decade.

Acquisition Theories

Theories of gender identity acquisition have informed different approaches to working with gender-expansive children. John Money, the psychologist who coined the term "gender" and theorized it as an identity distinct from biological sex, studied intersex children and observed the ways in which gender is, at least in part, socially constructed. He and psychologists Joan Hampson and John Hampson conducted research on children whose "sex of rearing" was the opposite of their biological sex. In an article that was published in 1955, Money and the Hampsons describe the case of one child with a condition called Congenital Adrenal Hyperplasia (CAH), which can cause the genitalia of children with XX chromosomes to appear masculine (Gill-Peterson 124). When the child was born, the attending doctors did not immediately assign a sex because the external genitals appeared ambiguous. After three days, the doctors told the parents that the child was a boy, so his parents raised him accordingly. The child received four genital reconstructive surgeries during his first three years to "correct" his inability to urinate while standing up. When he was three years and seven months old, it was determined that the child was actually biologically female, and he was diagnosed with CAH. His parents brought him to Harriet Lane Home, where Money conducted a psychiatric evaluation. The child exhibited significant distress when he thought that his examiners intended to surgically remove his masculine-appearing genitals. He also unequivocally referred to himself as a boy. From this study, Money defined "gender role" as follows:

> all those things that a person says or does to disclose himself or herself as having the status of boy or man, girl or woman, respectively [...] A gender role is not established at birth, but is built up cumulatively through experiences encountered and transacted—through casual and unplanned learning, through explicit instruction and inculcation, and through spontaneous putting two and two together to make sometimes four and sometimes, erroneously, five. In brief, a gender role is established in much the same way as is a native language. (285)

The fact that the first account of gender identity acquisition compares it to learning a native language suggests that these two processes are congruent in structure. Subsequent social learning theories of gender development, most notably Kay Bussey and Albert Bandura's, use the language of "models," "patterns," and "teaching" to describe how children develop gender identities . Writing center scholars also use this vocabulary to describe their understanding of language acquisition.

The authors of "Students' Right to Their Own Language," an influential statement that appeared in *College Composition and Communication* in 1974, noted that, despite the ambiguity present in research about how children learn languages, it is known "that children at very early ages begin to acquire performance skills in the dialect(s) used in their environment, and that this process is amazingly rapid compared to many other types of learning" (*CCC* 6). Further, they note:

> Dialect switching [...] becomes progressively more difficult as the speaker grows older. As one passes from infancy to childhood to adolescence and to maturity, language patterns become more deeply ingrained and more a part of the individual's self-concept; hence they are more difficult to alter. (*CCC* 8)

Similarly, Money claimed that a person's gender role "is so well established in most children by the age of two and one-half years that it is then too late to make a change of sex with impunity" (290). The learning model suggests that children learn patterns of language and gender behavior very early on, and, after these patterns are learned, they are difficult to "unlearn" or "relearn."

Understanding ingrained patterns in students is a crucial component of scholarship about tutoring multilingual writers. In his foundational text, "Cultural Thought Patterns," Robert Kaplan attempts to diagram the "movement" of paragraphs written by multilingual writers from different cultural contexts. He argues that "Logic (in the popular, rather than the logician's sense of the word) which is the basis of rhetoric, is evolved out of a culture; it is not universal. Rhetoric, then, is not universal either, but varies from culture to culture and even from time to time within a given culture" (2). Ilona Leki builds on Kaplan's work to argue that "different cultures do present written ideas in different ways, that members of a culture internalize those patterns of development, and that students transfer what they know about one writing situation to another" (92). In this way, as Leki notes, rhetorical logic is both socially constructed and firmly embedded in students. The task of writing center tutors is not to dislodge these patterns, but rather to help writers identify them and cultivate what is creative and compelling in their writing. As we shall see, this stance is similar to that of contemporary clinical psychologists who work with transgender and gender-expansive people.

Comparing Practices

Though these theoretical models of language acquisition and gender identity development have remained relatively stable over the past fifty years, there has been much debate within communities of writing tutors and clinical psychologists about "best practices." Carol Severino distills three distinct approaches to working with multilingual writers in her article "The Sociopolitical Implications of Response to Second-Language and Second-Dialect Writing." She calls these the "separatist," "assimilationist," and "accommodationist" stances. I see several parallels between Severino's tripartite model and different clinical approaches to working with gender-expansive and transgender young people. I also observe that the Gender Affirmative Model of care includes nuances for which Severino's framework fails to account. This section compares the practices of writing centers to those of gender identity clinics.

Severino defines separatism as "the belief that cultures, languages, and dialects in contact should be able to exist almost independently—unaffected, untainted by mainstream cultures, languages and dialects" (338). In this view, the tutor attempts to "preserve and celebrate linguistic diversity," which means that they make few interventions in the actual mechanics of the writer's writing, focusing instead on helping the writer develop their ideas (339). She associates this stance with the *CCC*'s "Students' Right to Their Own Language." More recently, Bruce Horner, Min-Zhan Lu, Jacqueline Jones Royster, and John Trimbur argued for a "translingual approach" to working with multilingual writers. This approach draws from the *CCC*'s statement and "sees difference in language not as a barrier to overcome, or as a problem to manage, but as a resource for producing meaning in writing, speaking, reading, and listening" (303). I place the translingual approach in the separatist category because its proponents also aim to "preserve and celebrate linguistic diversity." The underlying belief of this approach is that there is no one "right" way to write in English—and, therefore, that U.S. society needs to become more amenable to different styles of writing.

The Gender Affirmative Model similarly asserts a rights-based framework. The authors of the 2018 publication that compiles the core tenets of the model state:

> we, as care providers, need to be able to reevaluate our social constructs of gender and sexuality within our cultural context and the positions we impose on children. We see gender identity and expression as a basic human right. GAM practitioners should remain open to fluidity and changes over time and listen closely to our children's best attempt to explain themselves and respond in an affirming way (Keo-Meier and Ehrensaft 15).

This position is strikingly similar to the *CCC*'s statement that they "affirm the students' right to their own patterns and varieties of language—the dialects of their nurture or whatever dialects in which they find their own identity and style" (1). For both groups, an individual's ability to authentically express their identity is fundamental to their well-being. For separatists, that a certain pattern of behavior—such as conventional masculinity and femininity, or so-called "standard" English—is dominant does not mean that it is "correct." These practitioners are pluralists who attempt to cultivate the particularities of each individual's expression.

Severino notes that there is a risk in taking a separatist stance. She writes, "[a]t their worst, separatist responses, forgiving or applauding deviations from Standard English rhetorical and grammatical patterns, inevitably set students up for a shock when the next teacher, tutor, or employer they encounter tends toward an assimilationist stance" (339). Overly permissive tutors may not prepare multilingual writers for individuals who demand a specific kind of English writing.

On the opposite end of Severino's spectrum are "assimilationists." These tutors want the writing of multilingual individuals "to smoothly blend or melt into the desired discourse communities and avoid social stigma by controlling any features that in the eyes of audiences with power and influence might mark a writer as inadequately educated or lower class" (Severino 338). It is true that we live in a world where certain kinds of writing are deemed better than others. Consider *The New Yorker*, *The Washington Post*, or *The Economist* and you will find similar, neatly packaged prose. Short, declarative sentences are interrupted only occasionally by literary flourishes. This is the kind of writing that gets people hired at top companies and accepted for desirable fellowships. For many, the assimilationist approach is utilitarian: tutors and teachers want their writers to have tools that will give them the freedom to do what they want.

Well-meaning though such assimilationists may be, their logic resembles that of most clinicians working with gender-expansive children until only recently. I have already mentioned George Rekers's disciplinarian approach to "correcting" the effeminate behaviors of young boys. More recently, Kenneth Zucker's "developmental, biopsychosocial model" was accepted best practice in gender identity clinics until a little less than a decade ago. Zucker, who was considered the leading expert on gender nonconformity in North America for decades, encourages parents of gender-expansive children to replace their preferred toys with gender "appropriate" ones, to limit their children's cross-dressing, and to engineer same-sex peer friendships. He believes that setting limits on the cross-gender behaviors of these children could reduce their feelings of gender dysphoria, as well as prevent "the attendant social ostracism that can ensue from [Gender Identity Disorder] persistence, the complexities of sex-reassignment surgery and its biomedical treatment, and [...] family psychopathology and stress, when it is present" (390). Like assimilationist writing tutors, clinicians who endorse behavior modification techniques believe in changing the individual to fit within the dominant social structure, rather than changing the social structure itself.

Despite holding similar beliefs about language and gender acquisition, assimilationists and separatists disagree about the extent to which outside interventions can change an individual's identity. Separatist writing tutors believe that patterns of language become more deeply embedded in the individual—and therefore more difficult to change—as they grow older. The same goes for gender-affirmative clinicians. In contrast, assimilationists and interventionist psychotherapists believe that regimented and disciplined practice can help non-normative clients develop more normative patterns of behavior; to their minds, doing so is simply a matter of willpower.

Fan Shen describes his apparently successful assimilationist project in composition classes in his essay "The Classroom and the Wider Culture: Identity as Key to Learning English Composition." Shen, who is originally from China, describes his process of forming an "English identity" during composition and literature courses at a U.S. college. He compares this process to playing "a 'game' similar to ones played by mental therapists:

> First I made a list of (simplified) features about writing associated with my old identity (the Chinese Self), both ideological and logical, and then beside the first list I added a column of features about writing associated with my new identity (the English Self). After that I pictured myself getting out of my old identity, the timid, humble, modest Chinese "I," and creeping into my new identity (often in the form of a new skin or a mask), the confident, assertive, and aggressive English "I." The new "Self" helped me to remember and accept the different rules of Chinese and English composition and the values that underpin these rules. (462)

Shen makes the comparison between his work and that of a psychotherapist. He identifies a list of desirable characteristics for his "English Self," as well as a list of undesirable characteristics associated with his "Chinese Self." Similarly, clinicians like Zucker and Rekers identify a list of undesirable "effeminate" qualities and a list of desirable "masculine" qualities in order to treat gender-expansive boys. In both cases, the goal is to habituate desired behaviors and "correct" when undesired habits surface. One troubling consequence of this approach is that it often causes the individual upon whom it is used to feel ashamed of their identity. In Shen's case, we see him describe his "Chinese Self" as his "old" and "timid" identity. Though he claims that his process was also one of "balancing" his new English Self with his old Chinese Self, it is clear that he conceptualizes these selves as distinct, and he seems largely to dissociate from his Chinese Self. Similarly, pro-intervention clinical psychologists often cause girls to feel ashamed of their "masculine" selves and boys to feel ashamed of their "feminine" selves. For example, Karl Bryant, a participant in an early research study that evaluated the effectiveness of gendered behavior modification techniques, told an interviewer, "[t]he study and the therapy that I received made me feel that I was wrong, that something about me at my core was bad, and instilled in me a sense of shame that stayed with me for a long time afterward" (Schwartzapfel). Shen does not explicitly describe his behavior replacement experience as shameful, but his negative characterization of his Chinese Self reflects Bryant's sense that a core part of him was deficient.

The "new skin" or "mask" that Fan Shen dons during his process of transfiguration all too closely resembles what child psychologist Donald Winnicott called the "False Self." This False Self is a defense mechanism that develops in a person's psyche when their "True Self" is under threat, such as when they are disciplined for behaving in ways that feel natural. Regarding the individual who develops a "False Self," others may perceive their "academic success [to be] of a high degree, and may find it hard to believe in the very real distress of the individual concerned, who feels 'phony' the more he or she is successful" (140). Winnicott writes, "When such individuals destroy themselves in one way or another, instead of fulfilling promise, this invariably produces a sense of shock in those who have developed high hopes for the individual" (144). In other words, Winnicott suggests that the mask of the "False Self" will inevitably crack, leaving the "True Self" vulnerable to the harsh judgements of others. The pressure to perform in inauthentic ways, whether in writing or in gender expression, has devastating effects.

Even so, the demands of the professional world call upon individuals to perform in highly specific ways. Severino proposes a third, "accommodationist" stance that appreciates the unique expressions of multilingual writers while also recognizing that some contexts demand certain styles of writing. This approach "includes students not giving up their home oral and written discourse patterns in order to assimilate, but instead acquiring *new* discourse patterns, thus enlarging their rhetorical repertoires for different occasions" (Severino 340). Tutors who take this approach attempt to reconcile their support for the non-normative writing styles of multilingual writers and their knowledge that readers may bristle when faced with writing that does not conform to their expectations. Accommodationists aim to add tools to the writer's toolbox, not take away what is already there.

I find Severino's accommodationist approach unsatisfying because of the way it frames the conflict between the individual writer and the broader social context. She describes the tutor's process of "emphasizing that certain discourse features are appropriate or inappropriate for certain occasions" and teaching multilingual students when "third-person-singular-present tense markers" are "acceptable" versus when they are "unacceptable" (340). Words like "inappropriate" and "unacceptable" reflect broader, and potentially constraining, writing norms. This is the same framing that clinicians like Rekers and Zucker used when describing the behaviors of gender-expansive children. In the social world, it is "inappropriate" and "unacceptable" for boys to be effeminate. Boys cannot wear dresses or talk about their love of baking because these behaviors do not conform to social scripts of masculinity. Girls cannot get buzz cuts or play football because these things are not ladylike. This circular reasoning reveals the arbitrariness of these norms. On the other hand, questioning them allows us to recast so-called deviant behaviors in a more positive light. By permitting multilingual writers' non-normative writing patterns solely out of their fear of contributing to linguistic imperialism, the accommodationist tutor remains blind to what is genuinely special about these individuals' writing. Similarly, clinicians who "accommodate," rather than affirm, the non-normative expressions of gender-expansive children fail to recognize that diverse gender expressions can be cause for celebration.

Unswayed by Severino's accommodationist approach, and cognizant that the separatist, translingual approach is not always practical, I turn to the Gender Affirmative Model for a different way of framing the issue—one I find to be more productive than the language of "accommodation."

Applying the Gender Affirmative Model to Writing Center Pedagogy

The Gender Affirmative Model resembles the separatist stance toward tutoring multilingual writers, but gender-affirming practitioners recognize that some social environments are hostile toward people who do not act in ways that are typically associated with their assigned sex. Because of this, they sometimes support transgender and gender-affirming young people in a process of creating a "gender-conforming" persona. The important distinction between this and Fan Shen's method is that the clinician and client consciously acknowledge that this persona is a defense mechanism, not an additional "self." The clinician expresses positive regard toward the gender-expansive young person's authentic expression, and they also equip this young person with tools that will keep them safe.

In *Transgender Emergence*, Arlene Lev acknowledges:
Depending on the nature of the child's needs, the safety issues inherent in the community, as well as the parents' ability to assimilate the necessary information to be supportive to their child, children can be encouraged to only cross-dress at home, wear unisex clothing, be monitored in their use of transgendered resources on the Internet, change their name to a more gender neutral

one, or explore their cross-gender identity while on vacation (346). While Lev asserts that the primary goal of gender-affirming clinicians should be to facilitate broader social change surrounding norms of gender, she understands that some families and communities may resist a child's gender-expansive behaviors. She suggests that clinicians can help young people identify contexts that are more favorable to their gender expressions, such as at home or travel. In spaces that are not safe, the clinician can support the child by making compromises, like adopting a more androgynous appearance or using a name that could belong to a person of any gender. These practices are different from Fan Shen's process of creating an "English Self" because both the clinician and the child are explicitly aware that these behaviors are *not* expressions of self. Furthermore, this is a *temporary* solution to protect the child until they can enter a community that is more affirming of their identity.

Authors of *The Gender Affirmative Model* make a similar recommendation for clinicians who see gender-expansive young people that live in non-affirming environments. They write that a clinician can help the child learn:

> to don a "costume" associated with the assigned sex and later cast off the costume and [resume] expressing their authentic self. By regarding the "costume" as simply an adaptive social performance for the benefit of others who [are] not yet enlightened about gender expansiveness, the child [can] maintain an integrated sense of self while staying connected to the family (McLaughlin and Sharp 170).

The clinician can work with the child to recognize this set of normative behaviors—this "costume"—as a performance that is distinct from their true self. While Fan Shen attempts to become the "English Self" mask he wears, the gender-affirmative clinician keeps the child grounded in knowing that the mask of normativity is a tool—a means to an end rather than an end in itself.

Likewise, writing center tutors can use an affirmative framework when they work with multilingual writers. This affirmative approach differs from the accommodationist approach because it sees constraining norms, rather than individual writers, as the problem. In this view, multilingual writers who can convey their ideas effectively through their writing do not produce "inappropriate" or "unacceptable" work, and they do not need to be "accommodated" by tutors. When a writing center tutor recognizes patterns in a student's writing that do not reflect conventions that are traditionally associated with "good" academic English writing, they can first ask themself whether the writing conveys what the writer intends. If it does not, the tutor might assist the writer with identifying vocabulary that does communicate the desired message, perhaps by encouraging the writer to circumnavigate the meaning using words with which they are familiar. But, if the original writing does communicate what the writer wants, the tutor can highlight and praise specific parts of the writing that are novel. Further, when asking questions about the multilingual student's writing, the tutor can take a stance of affirming curiosity, rather than of accusatory interrogation. Just like gender-expansive expression, an expansive approach to English writing styles reflects human diversity and promotes positive recognition.

Even so, it remains true that too many people see diversity as an obstacle. In cases in which multilingual writers must enter a workspace, educational environment, or other social setting with people who stigmatize "non-standard" English writing, it may behoove the multilingual writer to craft a "standard" English "costume," just as a gender-expansive individual in a hostile place might do with a gender-normative mask. When the tutor works with the writer to create this costume, they should remind the writer about the creative and aesthetically unique aspects of their writing style. They should also assure the writer that the goal is not to become the costume, but rather use it to pass through spaces without being scrutinized. For example, a tutor might point out a non-normative writing pattern and say, "This is a great way of expressing your thoughts, and I want you to hold on to this. To get the fellowship you're applying for, the application reviewer might want you to write it a different way. I think that is unfair, so I want to give you the option of whether you want to play the role of their ideal applicant in your writing." The tutor might even help the writer do a "character study" of the "ideal" writer that certain readers are looking for by examining the writing of such people and inviting the writer to mimic them. The point of this practice is to simultaneously affirm the multilingual person's writing and to give this person an idea about the kinds of writing that people in different contexts value. Again, the tutor should not instruct the multilingual writer to construct an inorganic "self," but rather support them in honing a performance that will allow the writer to accomplish their goals. Moreover, the tutor should remind the writer that this performance is meant to be temporary, not a permanent replacement for the writing style that feels most natural to them.

Conclusion

Without diverse varieties of English, we would not have Zora Neale Hurston's *Their Eyes Were Watching God*, Virginia Woolf's *To the Lighthouse*, James Joyce's *Finnegan's Wake*, Toni Morrison's *The Bluest Eye*, or Chimamanda Ngozi Adichie's *Half of a Yellow Sun*, to name a few of many highly acclaimed literary works written in "non-standard" English. Teachers and tutors do a disservice to multilingual writers and to the broader concept of what constitutes "good" English writing when they take an assimilationist approach. And yet, we live in a society that is built upon highly technical policy memos, specifically constructed grant proposals, and a seemingly never-ending stream of applications whose reviewers demand conventional English writing. Writing center tutors must acknowledge both truths and grapple with how to proceed.

I have argued in this essay that gender is a useful analogy for understanding writing, and that gender-affirmative psychotherapy provides a generative framework that tutors can use when working with multilingual writers. Rather than taking a "separatist," "assimilationist," or even "accommodationist" approach, I have advocated for tutors to adopt an "affirmative" orientation. This stance sees the myth of "standard" English, rather than the different writing styles of multilingual writers, as a significant issue demanding attention. Just as gender-expansive and transgender individuals deserve to be lovingly recognized, people whose English writing is expansive in nature deserve the space to develop their voices and projects uninhibited by arbitrary norms. While we advocate for all teachers, employers, and readers generally to accept this truth, writing center tutors can help multilingual writers cope by teaching them to mimic normative writing styles when the situation demands it. Tutors and writers must do this while keeping their eyes lifted toward a future world that celebrates all forms of human expression.

Works Cited

Arlene Istar Lev. *Transgender Emergence: Therapeutic Guidelines for Working with Gender-Variant People and Their Families*. Haworth Clinical Practice Press, 2004.

Bussey, Kay, and Albert Bandura. "Social Cognitive Theory of Gender Development and Differentiation." *Psychological Review*, vol. 106, no. 4, 1999, pp. 676–713, https://doi.org/10.1037/0033-295x.106.4.676.

Conference on College Composition and Communication. "Students' Right to Their Own Language." *College Composition and Communication*, vol. 25, 1974, https://prod-ncte-cdn.azureedge.net/nctefiles/groups/cccc/newsrtol.pdf.

Gill-Peterson, Julian. *Histories of the Transgender Child*. University Of Minnesota Press, 2018.

Hidalgo, Marco A., et al. "The Gender Affirmative Model: What We Know and What We Aim to Learn." *Human Development*, vol. 56, no. 5, 2013, pp. 285–290, https://doi.org/10.1159/000355235.

Horner, Bruce, et al. "Language Difference in Writing--toward a Translingual Approach." *College English*, vol. 73, no. 3, 2011, pp. 303–321.

Kaplan, Robert B. "Cultural Thought Patterns in Inter-Cultural Education." *Language Learning*, vol. 16, no. 1-2, 1966, pp. 1–20, https://doi.org/10.1111/j.1467-1770.1966.tb00804.x.

Keo-Meier, Colt, and Diane Ehrensaft. "Introduction to the Gender Affirmative Model." *The Gender Affirmative Model: An Interdisciplinary Approach to Supporting Transgender and Gender Expansive Children*, by Colt Keo-Meier and Diane Ehrensaft, American Psychological Association, 2018.

Leki, Ilona. "Twenty-Five Years of Contrastive Rhetoric: Text Analysis and Writing Pedagogies." *TESOL Quarterly*, vol. 25, no. 1, 1991, p. 123, https://doi.org/10.2307/3587031.

McLaughlin, Robert J., and Robbie N. Sharp. "Working With Parents and Caregivers When Conflicts Arise." *The Gender Affirmative Model: An Interdisciplinary Approach to Supporting Transgender and Gender Expansive Children*, by Colt Keo-Meier and Diane Ehrensaft, American Psychological Association, 2018.

Money, J., et al. "Hermaphroditism: Recommendations Concerning Assignment of Sex, Change of Sex and Psychologic Management." *Bulletin of the Johns Hopkins Hospital*, vol. 97, no. 4, Oct. 1955, pp. 284–300.

Rekers, George A., and O. Ivar Lovaas. "Behavioral Treatment of Deviant Sex-Role Behaviors in a Male Child." *Journal of Applied Behavior Analysis*, vol. 7, no. 2, 1974, pp. 173–90. doi:10.1901/jaba.1974.7-173.

Severino, Carol. "The Sociopolitical Implications of Response to Second Language and Second Dialect Writing." *Journal of Second Language Writing*, vol. 2, no. 3, Sept. 1993, pp. 181–201. doi:10.1016/1060-3743(93)90018-X.

Shen, Fan. "The Classroom and the Wider Culture: Identity as a Key to Learning English Composition." *College Composition and Communication*, vol. 40, no. 4, Dec. 1989, p. 459. doi:10.2307/358245.

Schwartzapfel, Beth. "Born This Way?" *The American Prospect*, 14 March 2013, https://prospect.org/power/born-way/. Accessed 5 September 2022.

Winnicott, Donald W. "Ego Distortion in Terms of True and False Self." *The Person Who Is Me*. Routledge, 2018. 7-22.

World Health Organization. *Gender and Health*. https://www.who.int/westernpacific/health-topics/gender. Accessed 13 May 2021.

Zucker, Kenneth J., et al. "A Developmental, Biopsychosocial Model for the Treatment of Children with Gender Identity Disorder." *Journal of Homosexuality*, vol. 59, no. 3, Mar. 2012, pp. 369–97. doi:10.1080/00918369.2012.653309.

—. "The DSM Diagnostic Criteria for Gender Identity Disorder in Children." *Archives of Sexual Behavior*, vol. 39, no. 2, Apr. 2010, pp. 477–98. doi:10.1007/s10508-009-9540-4.

6 Utilizing Writing Center Pedagogy to Improve Communication in Healthcare for Limited English Proficiency Patients

Melissa Abel

Abstract

Healthcare is a fundamental human right, and I hope to use this paper to draw attention to the fact that, even with access to interpreters, patients who do not speak English are at a disadvantage in the U.S. healthcare system. All patients deserve high quality medical care that does not violate their autonomy, and, as a future medical professional, I believe we should search for solutions to this problem across disciplines. This project from ENWR 3620 highlights situations that I face daily while working and volunteering in healthcare, and it explains how those situations intersect with my academic work in a seemingly unrelated field. I believe that writing center pedagogy, while vastly different from medicine on the surface, may offer strategies that provide healthcare solutions.

Imagine you are scheduled for a heart stress test at your local hospital. This simple procedure is essential for your doctor to diagnose and treat a potentially life-threatening heart condition you may have. Now imagine that you are a non-native English speaker. A day before your appointment, you are called by an automated reminder system informing you of the details in robotic English that you can't understand. Not realizing that the recording eventually may repeat the message in your native language, you hang up. The night before your procedure, a nurse from the cardiology lab calls you using an interpreter service. While you can understand the interpreter, the meaning of a question you ask the nurse is lost in translation. The question remains unanswered. The day of the appointment arrives. The clinic maps are in English, and the staff at the information desk are unable to understand your request for directions. You finally make it to your appointment and have the test done. Your doctor decides to hospitalize you for overnight monitoring. The nurse has a busy shift and forgets to bring you a menu or patient guide in your language, so you do not know how to request food or speak to anyone about your stay. The interpreter can visit you once when the doctor arrives, but most of the time your nurses must use a phone-based interpreter system.

The United States has one of the largest populations of immigrants in the world – at 44.8 million people, or 13.7% of the U.S. population in 2018 (Budiman et al.). According to the 2009-2013 U.S. census, there are 16,344,437 people in the United States who speak English "less than very well" (US Census Bureau). Additionally, the authors of "Should All U.S. Physicians Speak Spanish?" write that, "according to the 2000 Census and the Bureau of Labor Statistics, the ratio of physicians to patients who speak English less than 'very well' is approximately 22:1" (Clarridge et al.), indicating that there is a need for interpreting services in hospitals. Unfortunately, even many major hospitals will not have enough properly trained and certified bilingual interpreters to attend to every non-English speaking patient. This shortage can result in devastating impacts on health outcomes and patient autonomy for non-English speaking patients.

In my position as a volunteer, non-medical Spanish translator at the University of Virginia Medical Center, I witnessed the struggles that both Spanish speakers and other non-English speakers face daily. My job responsibilities typically included visiting Spanish-speaking patients in their rooms, ensuring they had a menu and patient guide in Spanish, bringing them enrichment materials in Spanish, and helping them communicate with nurses. In addition to my patient-facing role, I helped with administrative duties in the language department. I made appointment reminder calls in Spanish, served as a translator between clinics and patients for cancellations and rescheduling, and used an interpreter service to call patients who speak languages other than English or Spanish.

When I started volunteering, I did not realize how impactful simple reminder calls could be to patients. The University of Virginia Medical Center, ranked among the best hospitals in the country, has a staff of only nine Spanish interpreters and one ASL (American Sign Language) interpreter, and it relies on volunteers for the reminder call service. Based on years of data, they have found that, without these reminder calls, the rate of no-shows to appointments increases dramatically. This comes at a cost to the hospital when a third-party interpreter is called in and not utilized, and it taxes an already busy language department staff, who must prioritize which patients receive in-person rather than phone translation.

In addition to helping the hospital and staff, reminder calls have a direct impact on patients. A few conversations I have had stand out in my memory. I helped a woman reschedule an appointment for an essential medical procedure at her gynecology clinic; she did not know how to use an interpreter to call the clinic herself. I called a man who spoke only Arabic and was unable to read or write; with the interpreters, we figured out a way to get him to his appointment. I helped a woman who had just lost her car to reschedule her appointment for a time when someone could drive her to the hospital. I spoke with concerned parents who learned, at the last minute, that the location of their child's appointment was in a clinic building instead of at the main hospital. Without volunteer reminder calls to get patients to the hospital, none of the other medical professionals would be able to help non-native English-speaking patients.

The experience I gained communicating with patients from other cultures has also prepared me to help them receive better medical care. I believe that if all people working in a medical setting were given a better understanding of the challenges that non-native English speakers face and equipped them with strategies for communicating more effectively, the medical field would provide a more positive experience to all patients.

Improved communication has implications not only for patient satisfaction but also for patient autonomy in decision making. As a student in ENWR 3620: Writing and Tutoring Across Cultures, the training class for writing tutors at the University of Virginia, I noticed a strong connection between the strategies we learned for working with multilingual writers and my experiences working with non-native English speakers at the hospital. That observation caused me to consider how strategies taught to tutors could be beneficial for front desk volunteers, physicians, and everyone else who hopes to provide improved care to patients with limited English proficiency.

Why Do Medical Providers Need Writing Center Strategies to Work with Patients with Limited English Proficiency?

Both provider-patient and tutor-tutee relationships rely heavily on interpersonal skills; in the medical field, this reliance can have significant consequences. After years of schooling and on-the-job training, it seems that healthcare providers should be well-versed in interacting with patients. With over sixteen million Americans unable to speak English well, it also seems that working with a translator should be routine. However, recent studies demonstrate that there is a need for further training of medical professionals who communicate with limited English proficiency patients.

Consider that effective provider-patient communication is crucial to maintaining an updated patient chart. Not only are patient charts "used for investigating serious incidents, patient complaints and compensation cases," but maintaining proper clinical records will "enable continuity of care and should enhance communication between different healthcare professionals" (Mathioudakis et al.). Patient charts are often shared between providers, and, when patients have multiple people working on their case, including doctors, surgeons, nurses, technicians, and therapists, the chart may be the only means by which some providers are able to communicate with others. Thus, proper charting is necessary to prevent miscommunication and needless repetition of tests and treatments (Mathioudakis et al.). One of the best practices when charting is to maintain an objective record of patient communication. This may include citing direct quotations from the patient, especially descriptions of their symptoms and questions they ask (Mathioudakis et al.). Without a shared language, there may be challenges in keeping objective medical records. Additionally, providers who don't understand the cultural and linguistic backgrounds of patients with Limited English Proficiency (LEP) can misinterpret patients' descriptions of their conditions. Even with a translator, the true meaning of a patient's words may be lost. In this case, it is important that providers utilize strategies to check understanding between themselves and their patients. Because any member of the healthcare team may be responsible for charting, all staff—regardless of position—should receive this training.

Maintaining a record of informed consent is another important provider-patient issue. Informed consent is "voluntary consent given by a person or a responsible proxy…after being informed of the purpose, methods, procedures, benefits and risks" of a medical procedure (Schenker et al.). This process requires a back-and-forth conversation between the provider and the patient to make sure that the patient knows exactly what a procedure entails before they agree to it. When working with patients who do not speak English, it is especially important that providers ensure that patients understand procedures. After such conversations, "documentation of informed consent is required […] at most hospitals in the United States and is a legal standard by which to judge whether informed consent has taken place" (Schenker et al.). Often:

> Full documentation of informed consent [requires] a procedure note documenting a consent discussion and a signed consent form. For [limited English proficiency] patients, full documentation additionally [requires] some evidence of interpretation. Acceptable evidence of interpretation [includes] one or more of the following: 1) documentation in the procedure note of a consent discussion in the patient's language or through an interpreter; 2) a consent form written in the patient's primary language; or 3) an interpreter's signature on the consent form. (Schenker et al.)

If these criteria are not met, a patient's autonomy in decision making may be violated. In the *American Journal of Bioethics*, Volandes and Paasche-Orlow write that "the autonomy of healthcare users with limited literacy is thwarted if the forms intended to preserve their individual autonomy are inaccessible." Forms written exclusively in English are inaccessible to patients with limited English proficiency.

Given the implications of informed consent documentation, one would expect consent to be well documented in patient charts, regardless of English proficiency. However, a case study at a teaching hospital in San Francisco found otherwise. The study analyzed the charts of patients who were either proficient English speakers or had limited English proficiency (LEP). The LEP patients spoke either Chinese (Cantonese or Mandarin) or Spanish. The researchers matched charts of English and LEP patients who had undergone the same medical procedure in the same area of the hospital during a similar time frame. The experimenters then reviewed charts "for documentation of informed consent (IC), including a procedure note documenting an IC discussion and a signed consent form. For LEP patients, full documentation of informed consent also included evidence of interpretation, or a consent form in the patient's primary language" (Schenker et al.). In their analysis, the experimenters found statistically significant evidence ($p = 0.003$) pointing to the following findings: English-speaking patients were more likely to have full documentation of informed consent than LEP patients, with 53% of English speakers having proper documentation and 28% of LEP patients having proper documentation (Schenker et al.). Patients of all languages were equally likely to have a procedure note mentioning that an informed consent discussion had taken place, but "only 41% of LEP patients had a consent form in their primary language or signed by an interpreter," and use of an interpreter was only documented for 22% of Chinese-speaking and 29% of Spanish-speaking patients (Schenker et al.). Given that the lack of a consent form in the patient's primary language indicates a violation of patient autonomy, this data has significant implications for the quality of care provided for all patients—especially for non-English speakers. Because only 53% of English-speaking patients had proper documentation of understanding in their medical record, it is evident that there is a communication and record-keeping problem in the medical field, not only for LEP patients, but for all patients. As such, patients may not always understand what they are consenting to before procedures.

Most medical professionals abide by a code of ethics, with physicians widely accepting the ethical concept called "medical professionalism." The American Board of Internal Medicine has defined medical professionalism as "not only [the physician's] personal commitment to the welfare of their patients but also collective efforts to improve the health care system for the welfare of society" ("Physician Charter"). The three main tenets of medical professionalism are patient welfare, patient autonomy, and social justice ("Physician Charter"). Patient autonomy is violated by a lack of informed consent, and, as discovered in the study by Schenker et al., nearly half of English speaking and ¾ of LEP participants did not have documentation of full informed consent. Stark differences between levels of informed consent in English and LEP patients speak to the code's social justice pillar. This disparity shows there is a need for reform to make healthcare more equitable for patients of all languages.

While this study only pertains to one hospital in the United States, it is a hospital that "has received several national awards recognizing the depth and quality of its interpreter services" (Schenker et al.). If this lack of documentation can happen at a hospital renowned for its interpreter services, it is highly probable that the same or worse could happen in a setting with fewer resources. Fortunately, writing center discourse provides concrete strategies for communication that could apply to the medical field and improve patient care not only for LEP patients, but for all patients.

What Writing Center Strategies Can Medical Providers Use to Improve Communication?

Having addressed challenges specific to healthcare providers, it is important to acknowledge the many similarities between tutoring a student and treating a patient. Though a tutoring session is not life or death, the listening and communication skills taught to prospective writing tutors could be incredibly beneficial to healthcare providers. In *The Oxford Guide for Writing Tutors*, Melissa Ianetta and Lauren Fitzgerald write, "empathy is especially important for writing tutors because writers sometimes share deeply personal matters […] this means that writers can feel vulnerable and even uncomfortable about sharing their work." A patient describing personal health concerns inevitably expresses vulnerability and needs a receptive and trustworthy audience in their provider. The *Oxford Guide* also suggests that writing is motivational, contending that "motivation is one of the greatest tools for acquiring new skills and knowledge" (Ianetta and Fitzgerald). Motivation is essential when medical providers are formulating plans for medication, therapy, rehabilitation, and a variety of other issues with patients whose care and health demand proactive attitudes. Many treatments—such as diets or at-home physical therapy routines—require determination from the patient to be successful. Additionally, just as a tutoring session is time-bound, an appointment is limited to a short period of time. Providers must be prepared to utilize this time effectively to provide information, treat problems, and address patient concerns. These direct similarities make tutoring strategies highly applicable to medical situations.

A tutoring session typically begins with an introduction between the tutor and tutee. *The Oxford Guide for Writing Tutors* recommends spending extra time talking in order "to get to know the writer and for the writer to get to know you," contending that such bonding "is essential to building a working relationship and getting the most out of your limited time together" (Ianetta and Fitzgerald). In the medical field, taking a few minutes to get to know a patient can improve the patient's experience by building trust and helping them feel comfortable sharing their concerns. As they do this, providers should pay attention to nonverbal cues from patients for any signs of discomfort and set expectations for what the patient will need to do to acknowledge their understanding; in other words, they should do just what the *Oxford Guide* instructs writing tutors to do (Ianetta and Fitzgerald). After this foundation of expectations and understanding is established, the provider can proceed with the appointment.

In order to prevent the problems associated with charting and informed consent discussed above, healthcare providers should adopt listening and questioning practices used by tutors. Indeed, Ianetta and Fitzgerald identify listening as "perhaps the most important of all the tutoring strategies," and it's critical for a tutor or provider to engage in active, rather than passive, listening. According to writing center scholar Frankie Condon, "active listening is saying back, in your own words, what you understand the writer to be saying" ("Strategies for Consulting"). Paraphrasing and mirroring back what the tutee says "lets [the writer] know that [the tutor] has heard and understood [them], but it also serves as a way to check perceptions and correct any possible misunderstandings" (Ianetta and Fitzgerald). If applied in medical contexts, the active listening strategy could help improve objective patient records. Through active listening, a healthcare worker could provide more accurate quotations in the chart or have a more precise understanding of what the patient means before paraphrasing their comments. When working with LEP patients, this strategy could help the provider resolve questions and answers that may have been lost in translation. Pointing is another strategy that could help clarify patient understanding and improve charting. In a tutoring session, pointing refers to the practice of "letting writers know which words, phrases, or images stand out" ("Strategies for Consulting"). While less directly connected to medicine, this strategy could identify primary concerns, symptoms, or sources of pain, based on what they have described. This practice would give the patient a chance to confirm or correct the provider's conclusions before recording the discussion.

    Questioning strategies can also be used to prevent misunderstandings. First, the provider can flip listening strategies back onto their patients. For example, they could ask patients to paraphrase instructions or information about a procedure back to them to check for understanding. This would help to ensure informed consent and, therefore, patient autonomy. Just as tutors are taught, providers should "ask follow-up questions that emphasize [their] curiosity and need to know" (Ianetta and Fitzgerald) to encourage dialogue with patients. Asking questions in a tutoring session allows "tutors and students to fill in their knowledge deficits and check each other's understanding," helping "tutors (and occasionally students) to facilitate [...] dialogue and attend to students' active participation and engagement" (Ianetta and Fitzgerald). The questions should be open-ended to "facilitate extensive and constructive responses," rather than cutting off conversation by asking a curt *yes* or *no* (Ianetta and Fitzgerald). Healthcare workers could apply similar methods and questions to encourage patients to provide thorough responses, contributing to a better foundation for patient education and objective charting.

    These listening and questioning techniques both have the potential to increase patient understanding and improve patient-provider communication. However, in the writing center, tutors serve as guides for their tutees not only about writing, but also about American culture. Tutors may help with "filling in information, closing background gaps, and helping international students find points of contact between their knowledge and experience and their assignments" (Severino). Healthcare providers may also play a similar role. For example, Spanish-speaking patients are one of the largest groups of LEP patients, with "64 percent of U.S. patients with limited English [speaking] Spanish" (Clarridge et al.). The Patient Centered Outcomes Research

Institute spoke with Hispanic men and women, finding that their medical concerns included "cultural sensitivity in health communications [… and] hesitation to take advantage of medical services, in part because of fears about immigration status or lack of insurance or other sources of payment […and] health literacy in Latino communities" (Harrah). In the face of such problems, it's worth restating the responsibility of every provider in contact with the patient to educate them about the healthcare issues that concern them. Just as tutors may fill in informational gaps for students, providers should do the same with cultural healthcare concerns for their LEP patients.

One way to begin addressing all these concerns is to gain a better understanding of the patient's culture. A perinatal services program manager in California stated, "knowing the culture, the customs, the religions [of patients] and trying to be sensitive to that is so important. It makes the patients feel like people" (Harrah). Severino writes that, in writing centers, "tutors need to learn from international students about their lives and cultures in order to tutor them better, and international students need to learn from tutors in order to perform better on their assignments. Thus, cultural informing is collaborative" (Severino). This mutual collaboration would only benefit medicine. The patient needs to learn about the American healthcare system and its traditions to make informed decisions about their health, and the provider needs to learn about the culture of the patient to identify their concerns and help them feel more comfortable in the American healthcare setting. At writing centers, this process can advance when tutors take "advantage of the visits of […] multilingual, multicultural individuals to the writing center and [show] interest in their home language, country, or culture by engaging them in the kind of small talk that usually accompanies tutoring sessions" (Leki). In the medical setting, this kind of progress can occur during the dialogue at the beginning of an appointment. I believe that the writing center strategies presented in this section would be appropriate and beneficial for use in the medical field to improve patient care, especially for LEP patients.

What Do We Do Now?

Throughout this paper, I have demonstrated that problems persist in healthcare with regards to patient-practitioner communication. These issues put the autonomy of patients at risk, and they are magnified for patients with limited English proficiency. However, strategies taught to writing center tutors can be used to address many of these problems. Given the wide variety of professionals who work with a single LEP patient and require clear and consistent communication about that patient's status, I believe this training would be beneficial for all workers in the healthcare setting. My personal experience as an administrative volunteer demonstrates this point, as even low-level, non-medical volunteers may face many interactions with LEP patients at every shift. The question arises, then: how should this training be delivered?

I propose that the training be presented upon hiring staff members and selecting volunteers at hospitals and clinics. Since curricula vary from school to school, I think that it would be both too difficult and insufficiently effective to implement this training in professional schools such as nursing, physician's assistant, and medical schools. Instead, hospitals would train their staff in these important interpersonal communication techniques. A local hospital or clinic will have a better knowledge of the LEP populations they serve and should thus oversee determining appropriate interventions and cultural exchanges, if necessary, for employee training. Teaching communication strategies could be achieved by inviting a local writing center professor or director to the hospital to teach new hires, or by having a staff member, trained as a tutor, isolate the strategies from writing center discourse that are most appropriate for the healthcare setting—as I have done in this paper. While this plan may not work in all medical settings, I hope that, by drawing a connection between medicine and writing centers, medical professionals will consider looking outside of their discipline for solutions to some of their most important communication challenges. All patients, regardless of their native language, deserve access to the rights and conveniences associated with open communication with their healthcare providers, and I believe the implementation of writing center tutoring strategies would provide just that.

Works Cited

Budiman, Abby, et al. *Facts on U.S. Immigrants, 2018: Statistical Portrait of the Foreign-Born Population in the United States*. The Pew Research Center, Aug. 2020.

Clarridge, Katherine E., et al. "Should All U.S. Physicians Speak Spanish?" *American Medical Journal of Ethics* , vol. 10, no. 4, Apr. 2008, pp. 211–216, journalofethics.ama-assn.org/article/should-all-us-physicians-speak-spanish/2008-04, https://doi.org/10.1001/virtualmentor.2008.10.4.medu1-0804.

Harrah, Scott. *Doctors & Diversity: Health Care for the Latino/Hispanic Population*. https://www.umhs-sk.org/blog/doctors-diversity-health-care-for-the-latinohispanic-population. Accessed 9 Dec. 2020.

Ianetta, Melissa, and Lauren Fitzgerald. *The Oxford Guide for Writing Tutors: Practice and Research*. Oxford University Press, 2016.

Leki, Ilona. "Before the Conversation." *ESL Writers: A Guide for Writing Center Tutors*, by Shanti Bruce and Ben Raforth, Heinemann, Feb. 2009.

Mathioudakis, Alexander, et al. "How to Keep Good Clinical Records." *Breathe*, vol. 12, no. 4, Dec. 2016, pp. 369–73. *PubMed Central*, doi:10.1183/20734735.018016.

"Physician Charter." *ABIM Foundation*, https://abimfoundation.org/what-we-do/physician-charter. Accessed 9 Dec. 2020.

Schenker, Yael, et al. "The Impact of Language Barriers on Documentation of Informed Consent at a Hospital with On-Site Interpreter Services." *Journal of General Internal Medicine*, vol. 22, no. 2, Oct. 2007, pp. 294–299. www.ncbi.nlm.nih.gov/pmc/articles/PMC2078548/, https://doi.org/10.1007/s11606-007-0359-1.

Severino, Carol. "Crossing Cultures with International ESL Writers." *A Tutor's Guide: Helping Writers One to One*, edited by Ben Raforth, Heinemann, Aug. 2005, pp. 41–53.

"Strategies for Consulting." UNL Writing Center, University of Nebraska, Lincoln, 2 Feb 2013, https://docs.google.com/document/d/1_SMcaYJTzdSJ8rcmQD7pXHI79enO_ziQCj2Tv1E8NnY/edit?usp=sharing.

US Census Bureau. "Detailed Languages Spoken at Home and Ability to Speak English." *The United States Census Bureau*, Oct. 2015, www.census.gov/data/tables/2013/demo/2009-2013-lang-tables.html. Accessed 9 Dec. 2020.

Volandes, Angelo E., and Michael K. Paasche-Orlow. "Health Literacy, Health Inequality and a Just Healthcare System." *The American Journal of Bioethics*, vol. 7, no. 11, 2007, pp. 5–10, https://doi.org/10.1080/15265160701638520.

7 From Speech Pathology to Writing Tutor

Kirsty Thompson

Abstract

This project addresses the links between the clinical field of Speech Pathology and writing center tutoring. Research methods incorporate writing center pedagogy from the course ENWR 3620: Writing and Tutoring Across Cultures, as well as speech therapy resources including clinical handbooks, articles written by certified Speech-Language Pathologists, and examples taken from professors in the Speech Communication Disorders Program at the University of Virginia. This project is intended to present writing center tutors, at UVA and beyond, with practical recommendations for approaching their tutoring sessions based on practices used in speech pathology.

Picture this: a small classroom, an awkward circle of those annoying swivel desk/chair combinations, a single podium with a computer. Nothing out of the ordinary, right? Now imagine that same room filled with college students from across the disciplines: a math major, computer science major, neuroscience major, French major, pre-med students, speech pathology students, among others. This combination is rare in most university settings because, not surprisingly, after completing their general education requirements, students usually take classes with peers who are in the same discipline and have professional goals that align with their own. This tendency makes a classroom like the one you just pictured unusual, or even intriguing; for students like me, that classroom was the locus of meaningful interdisciplinary overlaps. That classroom was where, in my second year at the University of Virginia, I took "Writing and Tutoring Across Cultures," a preparatory class for future writing center tutors. The course focused specifically on working with multilingual writers, and students were also required to volunteer through an engaged learning component that allowed us to transform our learning into community activism.

The decision to enroll in a training course and become a writing center tutor is not always an easy one. For example, upon first encountering course material such as Stephen North's "The Idea of a Writing Center," a critical piece of scholarship in the field with an off-putting and negative tone, many students were unsure whether they belonged. Amid the cloud of doubt that flooded our classroom during the first few weeks, students asked themselves whether, instead of becoming writing center tutors, they should be taking an important requirement for their major, spending their time at an internship, scribing at the hospital for medical school, or completing data science research. However, slowly and surely, each individual student began to discover how their particular disciplinary knowledge would contribute to the development of their writing tutor practices, helping them to find their place in this unique field. As a student of speech pathology, I discovered that my future profession had the potential to contribute significantly to the development of my own writing tutor practices, and potentially those of others. The moment I recognized the special way that my discipline could translate into writing tutor practices, I suddenly felt as if I belonged in that unique classroom.

For this reason, this piece will explore how skills and techniques from the field of speech pathology can inform and guide the practices of writing tutors. In the field of speech pathology, trained clinical professionals work in a wide array of settings including schools, private practices, skilled nursing facilities, and hospitals to diagnose, treat, and help to prevent speech, language, communication and swallowing disorders in children and adults. Some of the problems these professionals treat include articulation, pragmatics, stuttering, voice disorders, and aphasia ("Who Are Speech-Language Pathologists"). Since speech therapy is a clinical practice, many people may imagine it as a rigid, structured, and inflexible process that practitioners apply uniformly for all patients. However, if writing tutors take a closer look at the methodologies of speech therapy, they will see that many attributes of this field can translate to tutoring, helping to create more effective and successful sessions.

In comparing speech therapy patients with students who come to the writing center, I am not suggesting that these students have "problems" that need to be solved or "writing disabilities" that must be fixed by the tutor. Instead, I look at how specific aspects of speech therapy—such as Functionalism, Evidence-Based Practice, seeing each client as a unique individual, focusing on the client's growth, developing relationships with the client, prioritizing self-care, and recognizing that not everything is a quick fix—can translate to and improve writing tutor practices. By drawing this parallel between fields, I argue that a writing center tutor should act as a "writing therapist," helping an individual become functional in diverse contexts and assisting them in their journey to improve their writing process by offering scaffolding and support. Empowered by practices drawn from a field not often associated with writing center pedagogy, tutors can become more well-rounded and knowledgeable.

This transformation—from writing center tutor to "writing therapist" for others—means taking on the responsibility of helping writers cultivate the power of language, a concept that Christina Murphy explains in her piece "Freud in the Writing Center: The Psychoanalytics of Tutoring Well." Murphy explores the unique relationship tutors have with writers, describing how sessions often mirror aspects of psychoanalysis. Murphy states:

> As psychotherapists or tutors, we share with those in our charge the responsibility that goes with being human. And in our very human roles, we share the powers of language to express emotions, to inspire creative thought, and to change perceptions of the self and others. We share the power of language to transform thought and being.

Via Murphy's explanation, we can see how tutors can enter the same vital position as speech pathologists, standing between the complex and powerful system we call "language" and the individuals who are experimenting with ways to harness its power to express themselves in the world.

By examining this unique tutorial situation from a new perspective, through the eyes of a speech pathology student, the following pieces of advice are meant to guide the development of individual writing tutor practices. This paper looks at the unexplored parallels between the two fields and suggests ways they can grow from one another.

Beyond the Therapy Room, Beyond the Writing Center

Try placing yourself in the position of a speech pathologist. An eighty-year-old male patient who recently had a stroke walks into your therapy room for his session. He is retired and lives with his wife of 55 years; prior to the stroke, he had a scheduled daily routine. He is well-loved and was once a lively and talkative man. He now struggles to produce individual words. As his speech pathologist, you would love to get him back to where he used to be in terms of his language capabilities, but you know this is virtually impossible. As his therapist, you must decide what to focus on in his therapy sessions so that you can provide him with the highest quality of life (Robey).

There is no simple answer to this problem, and the conclusions that speech pathologists reach will vary from individual to individual, based on their unique life situations. In some cases, the patient can express their specific goals for the therapy and what capabilities they need to achieve for an improved quality of life. For example, the previously mentioned stroke patient might mention that he eats dinner out with his wife at the same restaurant every Friday night, so he would like to be able to order meals for both him and his wife—their tradition for years. This specific Activity of Daily Living (ADL) is something that this patient highly values, so the loss of this capability has altered his self-confidence: he feels that the stroke robbed him of acting like a gentleman for his wife. After this conversation with the patient, the speech therapist might go to that specific restaurant, ask for a menu, work on specific sentences based on the menu within the therapy sessions, and (eventually) go eat a "practice meal" with the patient to evaluate the fluidity of the social situation for which they have been preparing.

The above scenario exemplifies the idea of "functionalism," a concept that is of crucial importance for speech therapists, and something that should be just as highly valued in writing centers. In speech therapy, functional treatment is defined as a "person-centered approach that uses a patient's own goals to improve their performance and meaning in life tasks" (Baar). It is one thing to help the client communicate fluidly within the therapy room or write confidently at a writing center desk; it is an entirely different, more meaningful achievement to help the client take the skills they have acquired into the real world or other discursive situations.

"Functionalism" takes Stephen North's foundational Writing Center Studies argument for "producing better writers, not better writing" a step further by addressing how tutoring experiences can make writers functional in all future writing assignments and in their daily educational lives (North). Like speech therapists, tutors should approach each session with a mindset that involves looking past the walls of the writing center, making decisions based on what they judge to be the most important take-aways for the individual's future writing experiences. Tutors may help cultivate this mindset by considering how speech therapists take their patients' lives outside of the therapy room into account, as well as how they alter their sessions to make the most meaningful difference based on this knowledge. Alred and Thelen recognize that "teaching students to write requires much more than teaching a canon of rules; it requires that we enable students to rehearse a variety of strategies and to try them out." This quotation emphasizes the fact that tutoring is not about explaining a rule once to fix one error and then letting the writer forget about it. Rather, tutoring is about adding to the repertoire of strategies that the writer will use in all future assignments. Tutors are in a position similar to that of speech therapists: they can empower tutees with tools that will improve their participation in all of life's scenarios. The goal is for the individual to leave their tutor or therapist behind and become completely independent in their use of this acquired set of tools.

In the context of a tutoring session, enacting Functionalism might look like demonstrating how to locate information about MLA citations in an online guide, asking the writer to repeat the steps back, and working together to create a correct citation. By using these techniques instead of simply correcting all the errors themselves, tutors will be more focused on the student as a whole writer and can better ensure that the time they spend in the tutorial relationship creates a positive impact outside the comfort of the writing center. Because time is so limited in tutoring sessions, tutors must be savvy in deciding what will be most beneficial for the future of the individual with whom they are working. For both the 80-year-old stroke patient and the student struggling with their MLA citations, the Functionalist approach can determine individual needs for therapy or tutoring sessions—even if that is not what they entered the session expecting.

Evidence Based Practice

According to the American Speech-Language-Hearing Association (ASHA), Evidence Based Practice (EBP) is the "integration of clinical expertise/expert opinion, external scientific evidence, and client/patient/caregiver perspectives" ("Evidence-Based Practice"). Although it may not immediately be clear how those elements relate to writing tutors, EBP actually holds great promise. Incorporating the kind of EBP that is promoted in the field of speech pathology into tutoring practices will involve the integration of knowledge from previous tutoring and observation experiences, with external writing center literature, and the individual writer's perspectives. This passage reminds tutors of the variety of perspectives, experiences, and opinions a tutor should consider when working with a writer. New tutors often feel overwhelmed with all the different kinds of "best practices" offered to them by literature, the methods they observe from other tutors and writing center directors, and the concepts that they learn in training. The truth is that, over time, every tutor develops their own unique practice based on their experiences, successes, and failures with writers. Evidence Based Practice affirms the empowered individualism of writing tutors and respects proven information as well as the perspectives of the writer.

The benefits of Evidence Based Practice in the field of speech pathology have been noted by many, including Ralf Schlosser, who explains that EBP "may help to improve clinical services, bridge the divide between research and practice, make clinicians more accountable, and reduce variation in service provision." Similar benefits may apply to writing centers, where an altered version of EBP could help to bridge the gap between what tutors learn in training and through literature versus what they experience when they begin working with writers. Many tutors are surprised when they go into a tutoring session prepared to put the general techniques they have learned into action but soon discover that every session is a dynamic situation that may demand more than what they have learned in training. For this reason, a revised EBP approach translated from speech therapy has the potential to empower tutors to do what they think best for writers while respecting the research and knowledge acquired by those with more experience. Although a writing tutor often must make decisions "on the fly" as they work with a writer, it is important to remember that, when making these decisions, they incorporate techniques from the literature and from their past experiences, all while respecting the writer's needs. Tutors can achieve this balance by examining how speech pathologists incorporate their professional knowledge, stay up to date with current research and successful new methods in the field, and recognize the perspectives of their patients.

In both disciplines, maintaining a balance between different sources of information can be challenging, but an examination of the use of the EBP statement in speech pathology shows how effective the writing center EBP statement could be in streamlining sessions and empowering tutors. Just as speech therapists "have a responsibility to use treatments that are backed by research" ("The Speech Pathologists Guide"), tutors have the responsibility to take heed of advice from writing center literature that has been proven to help individual students. Just as speech therapists "have to use their own clinical expertise to judge the validity of evidence" ("The Speech Pathologist's Guide"), tutors must use their past tutoring experiences and observations to judge perceived effectiveness of possible pedagogies. Lastly, and most importantly, just as therapists must "factor the client into their clinical discussion" ("The Speech Pathologist's Guide"), tutors must pay attention to the writer as an individual, collecting information about the writer's preferences, background, and writing experiences in order to decide which methods will be the most advantageous.

To make this complex connection clearer, let's examine a scenario in speech pathology in which a therapist utilizes EBP. The parent of a child with a Spoken Language Disorder (SLD) seeks treatment to improve their child's pragmatics and semantics. Based on the young age of the child and their current language capabilities, the therapist evaluates peer-reviewed research and current best practices and decides to take the Pivotal Response Treatment (PRT) approach. This approach is a "play-based, child-initiated behavioral treatment," which has goals of "teaching language, decreasing disruptive behaviors, and increasing social, communication, and academic skills" ("Spoken Language Disorders"). The therapist then reevaluates this method of treatment based on their professional experience. However, the process does not end there. Finally, the therapist then integrates the client's and parents' feedback.

Due to the nature of tutoring writers, all these complex processes integral to speech therapy must be condensed, and decisions are often made based on "thin slicing," a concept explained by Malcolm Gladwell in *Blink* and advocated for by writing center scholars (Geller et al.). Gladwell defines "thin slicing" as "the human capability to use limited information from a very narrow period of experience to come to a conclusion." Gladwell suggests that spontaneous decisions can be just as good as, or sometimes better than, carefully planned ones. This concept applies to tutoring that uses EBP because it indicates that tutors can develop intuitive judgment via training, experience, and knowledge. Although Gladwell argues that spontaneous decisions can be of the same quality as thoroughly planned ones, he also recognizes that these decisions are made based on professional experience, research, and client perspectives—the same things that are included in the writing center EBP statement. Thus, although tutors often make decisions "on the fly," they must prepare for these spontaneous moments by staying up to date on literature, pedagogy, and advice from peers, just as speech pathologists do.

Relating to the Individual

For years, speech therapists have used music to create more engaging, less stressful, and more effective experiences for patients. Music is a universal language that has the power to speak to a patient's soul, no matter the patient's age, and certain songs can even change their outlook on a situation. The significance of the "certain songs" component of that statement is that the music that a therapist decides to include in therapy must align with the culture, past experiences, and preferences of their patient to be effective. For example, an elderly patient will likely only respond positively to the original artist and original recording of a song that they listened to in their youth; a cover or re-make just won't "do it" for them because it does not have the same power to transport them back in time. For this reason, the speech therapist must invest significant time in getting to know their patient as an individual.

The story of a man named Henry, who existed in a solemn state in an assisted living facility due to medical conditions and the inability of his family to consistently care for him, provides an example of the significant impact of incorporating music in speech therapy. All the staff in the facility knew Henry to be perpetually hunched over with his head down, only mumbling in response to people talking to him. However, once the staff learned what kind of music Henry listened to in his youth when going dancing, they played it for him through a headset, and he immediately lit up and started singing. Henry went on to share countless stories about his "other life." He had been nervous to talk in front of others because of his speech difficulties, but something about the music brought him out of his shell and transformed him into the joyous man that his family knew and loved.

The key lesson here is that the music Henry heard was only effective in encouraging him to speak, or sing, because of questions the nursing staff asked about his preferences as well as the genuine interest they showed in his life experiences. This speech therapy practice of paying special attention to the client as an individual and adapting the treatment to their needs applies to tutoring as well. Many of the papers that writers bring to tutoring include references to past experiences, languages, and cultures with which the tutor may be unfamiliar. To better understand a writer and assist them in the writing process, the tutor must learn about the background of the student by asking questions and by being genuinely interested in the ways their writing represents their individuality. In Severino's "Crossing Cultures with International ESL Writers," she states that tutors and writers should be prepared to "converse about perceptions of cultural differences and build toward a mutual understanding," and she also goes on to say that tutors need to act as "cultural informants" who help their writers find points of contact between themselves and their often US-based writing assignments. Tutors can play this important role of cultural informant by following in the steps of speech pathologists, who actively engage with the experiences, cultures, linguistic histories, and opinions of their patients to create the most effective therapy.

In tutoring, this might take the form of digging deeper into a cultural reference or description mentioned in a writer's piece. Instead of making the simpler choice and skipping past such moments, tutors act as cultural informants who find points of contact with US culture. For example, if a writer is describing the concept of a mother's love in an assignment that is supposed to be an argumentative essay, the tutor could take a contrastive rhetorics approach, examining the student's technique alongside the expectations of American academic writing. An important notion for tutors to remember when discussing cultural differences with writers is that every writer is unique; tutors should never generalize about cultural groups, race, or ethnicity.

The uniqueness of every client and session is another example of how the dynamic nature of tutoring sessions parallels speech therapy. Tutors must recognize this diversity and learn to invest time in learning about each individual so that they can better understand their rhetorical decisions and relationship to writing. Especially when working with multilingual writers, the tutor should build a relationship with the writer by asking questions and being genuinely interested in their history and past experiences. This curiosity reflects the techniques that speech pathologists use to correctly implement a therapy practice, such as playing music to engage a patient. By acquiring knowledge about the individual with whom they are working, they can make individualized decisions. In a similar fashion, to help a writer become more functional, tutors must engage with the individual's experiences and culture to explore their rhetorical decisions and thereby act as a cultural informant. To do this, tutors should enter each session empowered by their experience, practice, and theoretical knowledge but also with a blank slate, wiped clean of all prejudice, stereotypes, and assumptions about their client.

Who Really Needs the Practice?

As a speech pathology student, I have listened to many anecdotes about professional speech therapy experiences from professors who were speech pathologists in their former lives. One story that has stuck with me is from Randall Robey, a professor in the Speech Communication Disorders department at the University of Virginia. When Robey was just out of graduate school, he felt well-armed with information and techniques for therapy sessions, and he was practically bursting with excitement to put all this new knowledge to work in his first position. However, due to this excitement and apparent wealth of knowledge, Robey spent many of his first therapy sessions talking "at" the patient: providing countless techniques, ideas, and advice while barely giving the patient any time to practice their speech and language skills themselves. One of his supervisors suggested that Robey record and review one of his sessions, which led to a discovery that altered the course of Robey's clinical career. With the guidance of his supervisor, he realized that the patient was the one who should be spending most of the session speaking and practicing the skills with which they struggle, but he was taking up all the patient's time doing the talking himself (Robey).

Young speech pathologists and tutors alike can learn from this story: after a tiring first few sessions going through papers, correcting all the small grammatical mistakes and making countless changes while the writer just sits there and watches their paper "improve," the tutor realizes that tutorials must be collaborative efforts. Just as Robey realized that his client was the one who should be practicing their speech and language, a writing tutor can realize that the tutee is the one who should be developing their skills and making discoveries about writing techniques during the session. The writing tutors must learn to take a step back from the position of "editor" and instead act as a guide in the writing process, suggesting techniques and offering options for improving the paper but ultimately leaving final decisions to the writer. Tutoring sessions should not be focused on achieving an "A" on the paper, even if that is why the student came to the writing center; instead, they should be focused on helping the student develop as a writer, learning new techniques that will allow their writing to improve exponentially in the future. Thus, tutors should keep themselves in check by continually asking themselves what Robey asked himself: "Who really needs the practice?" If a writer does not have the chance to enact the tools they encounter during the session, it is essentially the same as a speech pathologist explaining the numerous ways a client could reduce their stutter, but not allowing the client to use session minutes to practice the sounds and phrases with which they struggle.

In a tutoring session, ensuring that the student is the one practicing their writing process may involve introducing them to the concept of the "author's note." By writing an author's note during a tutoring session, the student can explore their purpose in writing the paper, the process they went through to reach the most recent draft, and the ideas that they feel are still a "work in progress." This is a way for the student to speak back to their own writing, meaningfully engage in their own writing process, and identify the rhetorical decisions that they make in their writing (without even noticing). This tutoring practice ensures that the student is the one developing as a writer, and it prevents the tutor from imposing their observations regarding the direction in which the paper should be—or has been—taken.

Tutor/Writer and Therapist/Patient Relationship

Both writing center tutoring and speech therapy are vulnerable situations for the individuals who seek help. The ability to express emotions, thoughts, feelings, and opinions through language, be it spoken or written, is fundamental for participation in society; a deficiency in one of these areas often presents an open avenue for self-consciousness and isolation. Speech therapists recognize the critical importance of the therapist-patient relationship and are always actively engaged in ensuring that it is honest, based on mutual trust, and that it exists within a safe environment. The tutor-writer relationship is similarly critical, but its importance is less commonly recognized or appreciated because tutors often work with an individual writer only once and then never see them again. This pattern creates the impression that there is not enough time to produce a meaningful relationship. However, a tutor can cultivate this special bond with a writer, even in a short period of time, by emulating speech therapy's tendency to value open relationships that prioritize opportunities for improvement.

In the first speech therapy session with a new patient, it is common practice to engage in normal, low-stress conversation—or to play a game with or introduce a toy to younger patients— to evaluate their preliminary speech abilities and begin molding the relationship. From the moment the patient walks in the door, their first impressions of the therapist and preliminary decisions about their potential relationship begin to take shape. Randall Robey has a uniquely straightforward approach to the challenge that these initial impressions pose, and he explains to future speech pathologists each semester that, during each initial session with a new patient, he sits down with them and explains that, for their therapy to be effective, the patient must trust him and be willing to make mistakes in front of him. He tells them, "This is our room, our space, and anything that happens within the confinements of these four walls stays between us. The only way for us to make progress is for you to be willing to make the mistakes that you often attempt to prevent in daily life" (Robey). For example, Robey would encourage a patient who stutters not to be afraid to do so in that room because the more stuttering that Robey is able to witness and evaluate, the more effective decisions how to structure therapy sessions. Speech therapists must have the opportunity to experience what their clients sound like in their daily lives, so that they can create effective treatment plans and evaluate the progress that therapy achieves.

Although a writer may not be willing to be totally vulnerable at the beginning of a tutoring session, the small-talk and preliminary conversations that tutors have with their tutees build the trust and foundations for profound relationships, whether those involved realize it or not. A writer will share their opinions and explore their process and rhetorical decisions aloud only if they are not afraid of judgment or rejection from the tutor. This writer-tutor relationship may be different than anything the writer has experienced, especially if they are an international student, which might mean that they are accustomed to teacher-student relationships in which they are told exactly what to do and provided with clear definitions of right and wrong. Pedagogical relationships differ greatly amongst cultures and regions, and being conscious of this diversity is key in a tutoring environment. In this regard, an efficient way to start a tutoring session is with an honest conversation similar to Robey's, in which the tutor explains that they are acting as a peer—someone on the same level—who is there to offer advice, but that, ultimately, the rhetorical decisions are up to the writer. This kind of upfront conversation, inspired by speech therapy, is a constructive practice that defines the relationship and clarifies both parties' expectations.

A discussion of session goals is, therefore, something tutors can take from the field of speech therapy; in this way, tutor and tutee can reach a mutually beneficial plan regarding how the session will progress. Speech therapists regularly outline goals for treatment clearly with the client, or their parents, as well as the steps they will take together to reach them. Kate Kostelnik, the professor of the training course mentioned at the beginning of this piece, provides an example of the way this practice can apply to tutoring writers. She initiates sessions with multilingual writers by explaining very clearly that they will not leave with a perfect paper because her goal is to help improve them as a writer, not to improve the paper (Kostelnik). Honest explanations like this are important for defining the writer-tutor relationship and for cultivating trust because they clarify expectations and provide guidance about how to approach the session.

Because they know how vital it is for the client to respect and interact honestly with their therapist, speech pathologists put a lot of effort into their patient relationships and are honest when they think that a relationship is not "clicking." Tutors must put the same effort into their own relationships because, although they may only work with a writer once, sessions will only be effective if the writer is willing to be vulnerable with their writing; they must feel comfortable placing significant trust in the stranger they met only moments before. To achieve successful relationships like those that speech pathologists hold with their patients, tutors can employ practices such as low-stress conversation, preliminary and/or continued dialogue about expectations, and other kinds of check-ins. This might look like the tutor relating to the stress that the writer is feeling as a student, sympathizing as the student deals with a particularly difficult assignment, or even just initiating a friendly chat about extra-curricular activities. Because this is a relationship that does not exist in many other academic settings, tutoring offers a unique opportunity for collaborative engagement on writing assignments. Other than peer reviews in classroom settings, peer-to-peer interactions like this can be rare. When they do occur, they offer many benefits; students are often far more comfortable expressing their stress and emotions to someone their own age, rather than to an intimidating professor. Tutors can take advantage of the unique qualities of these relationships to help writers transform.

Not Forgetting About Your Own Self-Care

Speech pathologists' co-workers, friends, and family often advise them to take time for themselves. This is good advice for people in all professions, but it is especially important in occupations that involve channeling all your energy and thought into others. Speech pathology is a selfless profession, but this means it can also be exhausting; improving a client's speech and language takes time, dedication, and persistence, and therapists do not always get the recognition they deserve or see the progress for which they hope. Tutors also experience exhaustion because they put just as much thought and effort into their writers' papers as they would put into their own academic assignments. Writing tutors can borrow certain practices from speech therapists that might help to alleviate these effects: actively participating in their disciplinary communities and with their peers, respecting the work-life balance, and leaving time for self-reflection.

Speech therapists are encouraged to participate in local, national, and global networks of professionals in the discipline, which can offer opportunities to give and receive help with particularly difficult cases, as well as provide other kinds of support. A similar sense of community is also evident in the writing center field: at conferences, tutors and writing center advisors discuss difficult sessions or issues they have encountered, collaboratively work through issues, and seek advice. However, these conferences are not always accessible to individual tutors, so, as the authors of *The Everyday Writing Center* suggest, tutors can also take a more local approach, creating a "community of practice" through a central journal or forum in which tutors from an individual writing center can communicate and express their concerns, challenges, or successes. A shared journal offers "frequent opportunities for genuine moments of discovery and invites the type of checking, confirming, and balancing that is at the center of tutor reflections" (Geller et al. 84). This kind of tutor-centered journal offers a more relaxed and free-form space, which differs from the session reports that tutors complete after each meeting with a writer, because it is not directed towards an academic audience or towards the center's directors, but rather towards peers. These journals provide a way to mimic speech pathologists' use of online forums, groups, and meetings to work through their sessions and emotions with others who can truly empathize with their experiences. Being actively involved in your local, professional community is a common practice in speech therapy, and it is another example of a takeaway for those in similar situations, such as writing tutors.

Respecting work-life balance—leaving work in the professional setting and not letting it monopolize mental space outside of that setting—can be a challenge for both speech pathologists and writing tutors. Both jobs often inspire an almost unstoppable passion for helping others and a desire to spend countless hours trying to make a difference in clients' lives. Due to the numerous obligations and responsibilities of a speech pathologist, it often seems as if their work is never finished, and they are constantly aware of more they can do for their clients. Speech pathologists are characteristically passionate about their profession, often going to extreme lengths for their clients. In one example, a speech language pathologist who saw patients, families and caregivers struggle to find real food options that were tolerable and satisfying went on to create an easy-to-swallow, dissolvable bar that "provides easy calories for children and adults who may have difficulty swallowing, a loss of appetite or taste, sensory issues or failure to thrive" (Dow). Likewise, it is often difficult for writing tutors to prevent themselves from adopting the stress and concern radiating from writers regarding their papers and grades. Since tutors are usually students themselves, it is easy to empathize with the writers' concerns about grades; they may be anxious to know if they did enough during the tutoring session, often curious about the grade the student received. The important thing for tutors to remember is that, once the session is over, they must accept that they did everything in their power to make the student a more confident and skilled writer. The moment that they step outside of the threshold of the writing center, they must return to their own academic lives and personal concerns. Speech pathologists see their patients more repetitively, so they practice this daily by ensuring that they leave their work where it belongs: in the clinic.

According to professional guidelines, "speech pathologists typically write diagnostic reports, therapy plans, progress reports, and discharge reports" for each patient (*Clinic Handbook: Speech and Language Pathology*). Although these clinical reports can provide one avenue for reflection on therapy sessions, they are not really about the feelings or attitudes of the therapist and are often a source of stress due to deadlines and the necessity for accurate reporting. As a result, speech therapists often find other avenues for relief and reflection—such as journaling, meditation, and down time. There are countless advice blogs written by fellow speech pathologists offering support to their peers' engagement in self-care in such a selfless profession. Although tutoring might not seem as selfless, it does involve putting remarkable effort into making a difference in students' writing lives. Especially with multilingual writers, the tutor's role may go beyond working collaboratively on a paper and involve complex positions such as cultural informant and friend. These roles can take a lot out of a tutor, so finding ways to relieve stress and take breaks are necessary. For example, to reduce stress and anxiety, tutors can practice mindfulness meditation before, after, and between sessions with writers, which is something that many speech pathologists do in their down time (James). Mindfulness is an effective way to regulate emotions, cultivate a beginner's mindset, and "reset" between therapy or tutoring sessions.

Attempting to Beat the Clock

Clients who seek out or are referred to speech and language therapy present a diverse array of disorders, the vast majority of which cannot be easily resolved. Sometimes this fact can be hard to accept for new speech therapists, especially when progress is slow or not clear. Speech therapy requires dedication, hard work, and commitment over an extended period from both the therapist and the patient to truly make a difference. Writing tutors must recognize and understand an analogous reality; tutors often feel as if they have made no progress with the writer during a session because they saw repetitive mistakes, because the writer did not seem engaged, or because they felt as if the working relationship was lacking in some way. Most centers designate that tutors work for thirty or sixty minutes with writers, which seems impossibly brief in comparison with the immense dedication tutors must make progress with their writers. The resulting stress from this pressure is reminiscent of the pressure that can occur in speech therapy, wherein family members, loved ones, and other medical professionals who care deeply for the patient desperately want to see immediate improvement. Tutors can therefore look through the lens of speech therapy to evaluate how therapists manage time constraints, outside pressure, and the frustration of slow progress.

The concept of "time" seems to be of critical importance in the minds of both speech therapists and writing tutors because it often feels as if they severely lack this resource when they have such a multitude of salient intentions. In *The Everyday Writing Center,* Geller et al. recognize that "society has become enamored with speed" and that "time often begins to function as an excuse" in modern society, and specifically in tutoring sessions (35). To address this challenge, writing tutors can observe how speech therapists learn to treat time as a friend, rather than as an enemy. Tutoring sessions—like therapy—should not be a rush against time to accomplish as much as possible but a process in which progress is allowed to expand and contract in a manner that is best suited to the individual writer. If a young speech therapy patient comes in having a temper tantrum because they were woken from a nap to come to therapy, the therapist does not become instantly concerned about the time they are "losing" due to the tantrum; instead, they adapt the session to the needs of their client. If this means spending ten minutes playing with a toy or talking about a movie the child saw that weekend, that's okay; those activities are opportunities to practice the patient's speech, and there's no need to fight desperately with the clock to follow a predetermined plan.

Tutors can adopt this practice of treating time as a "friend" by accepting whatever situations arise and adapting their methods to fit writers' needs. For example, if a writer comes in panicking with two hours left before a deadline, instead of turning them away, the tutor takes a deep breath and has a calm discussion with the writer to reach a mutual decision about the best way to spend the time they have together. Instead of fretting about how they will not be able to fit in all the intricately planned, well-thought-out steps they normally follow with writers, the tutor accepts the time limit, appreciates the experience, and makes the best of it. Appreciable success and learning can come from challenging tutoring sessions, ones that make the tutor question their regular practices and move towards unexpected, but rewarding, new techniques. By mimicking the quality of adaptability that many speech therapists possess, writing tutors can also learn to befriend time and work through challenges with level heads and open minds.

Another problematic assumption that many tutors have is that a "quick fix" is all that is required to make fundamental change in a writer's process and rhetorical decisions. Both improving writing and treating speech and language disorders involve gradual changes and extreme diligence. Tutors can learn to adopt the self-empowering mindsets that many experienced speech pathologists develop, which involve taking things slowly, accepting that progress is not always visible, and simply doing their best to gradually equip their clients with the tools they need to improve. Especially when a tutor may only work with a writer once, they must learn that the best way to evade doubts following their sessions is to put all the powerful tools they have gained to use during the session, and afterwards reflect that they did everything they could.

Moving Forward as a Writing Therapist

I truly hope that these practices and scenarios from speech therapy contribute as powerfully to the writing tutor practices of others as they have to my own. The overlap between these two fields has the potential to alter writing tutor practices for the better, and, on the other side of the transfer, writing tutoring has the potential to contribute meaningfully to speech pathology. I am grateful for the opportunity to explore this interdisciplinary interaction and for the chance to be an active participant in both selfless and change-making jobs. Writing tutors, or, perhaps, writing therapists, and speech pathologists both play such important roles in the lives of their clients.

Works Cited

Alred, Gerald J., and Erik A. Thelen. "Are Textbooks Contributions to Scholarship?" *College Composition and Communication*, vol. 44, no. 4, Dec. 1993, p. 466. https://doi.org/10.2307/358382.

Baar, Sarah. "Speech Therapy Resources for Functional Cognition Treatment: A Person-Centered Approach." *SpeechTherapyPD*, 4 July 2019, www.speechtherapypd.com/single-post/2019/06/26/Speech-Therapy-Resources-For-Functional-Cognition-Treatment-A-Person-Centered-Approach.

University of Maryland Department of Hearing and Speech Sciences. *Clinical Handbook: Speech-Language Pathology*. 2017. https://hesp.umd.edu/sites/hesp.umd.edu/files/handbook_2017 2018_word_final_final_pdf_4.pdf

"Speech Pathologist Creates Snack for People Who Have Difficulty Swallowing." *Cision PR Newswire*, 5 Mar. 2019, https://www.prnewswire.com/news-releases/speech-pathologist-creates-snack-for-people-who-have-difficulty-swallowing-300806411.html

"Evidence-Based Practice (EBP)." *American Speech-Language-Hearing Association*, https://www.asha.org/research/ebp/evidence-based-practice/. Accessed 4 Nov. 2019.

Anne Ellen Geller, et al. *Everyday Writing Center a Community of Practice*. Utah State UP. University Press, 2007.

Gladwell, Malcolm. *Blink: The Power of Thinking Without Thinking*. Little, Brown, and Co., 2005.

James, Melissa. "9 Self-Care Tips for the Time-Crunched Audiologist or SLP." *Leader Live — Happening Now in the Speech-Language-Hearing World*, 29 June 2017, https://leader.pubs.asha.org/do/10.1044/9-self-care-tips-for-the-time-crunched-slp/full/.

Murphy, Christina. "Freud in the Writing Center: The Psychoanalytics of Tutoring Well." *The Writing Center Journal*, vol. 10, no. 1, 1989, pp. 13–18. JSTOR.

North, Stephen M. "The Idea of a Writing Center." *College English*, vol. 46, no. 5, Sept. 1984, p. 433. doi:10.2307/377047.

"Old Man in Nursing Home Reacts to Hearing Music from His Era." *YouTube*. https://www.youtube.com/watch?v=NKDXuCE7LeQ. Accessed 6 Nov. 2019.

Robey, Randall. "Basics of Clinical Practice." University of Virginia, 18 April 2019, Charlottesville, VA, EDHS 2450 Lecture.

Schlosser, Ralf W. *The Efficacy of Augmentative and Alternative Communication*. Academic Press, 2003.

Severino, Carol. "Crossing Cultures with International ESL Writers." *A Tutor's Guide: Helping Writers One to One*, 2nd Edition, Boynton/Cook Publishers, pp. 41–51.

"Spoken Language Disorders: Overview." *American Speech-Language-Hearing Association*, https://www.asha.org/Practice-Portal/Clinical-Topics/Spoken-Language-Disorders/.

"The Speech Pathologist's Guide to Evidence-Based Practice." *Speech Pathology Master's Programs*, https://speechpathologymastersprograms.com/evidence-based-practice/. Accessed 15 Nov. 2019.

"Who Are Speech-Language Pathologists, and What Do They Do?" *American Speech-Language-Hearing Association*, https://www.asha.org/. Accessed 18 Nov. 2019.

8 The Negative Implications of Western-Centric Scientific Writing Guidelines and a Solution for Struggling Scientists

Tanvika Vegiraju

Rigid guidelines for scientific writing have caused scientists to encounter emotional and psychological barriers to reporting their findings. Some scientists have difficulty expressing themselves or finding their voice, and many lack sufficient access to resources or training in scientific writing genres, finding it difficult to follow imposed and seemingly arbitrary rules. Consequently, Western-centric scientific writing guidelines have resulted in the exclusion of the ideas of brilliant scientific minds.

Biologist Kaj Sand-Jensen has offered similar critiques, arguing that the "allure of enthusiasm [in research] is often lost in the predictable, stilted structure and language of scientific publications." The main issues he raises with current scientific writing conventions are the exclusion of implications and speculations, the tendency to avoid originality and personality, and the omission of necessary steps of reasoning. He argues that though these ideas and approaches are discouraged, they are essentially what bring innovation into the scientific field.

For example, although speculation is heavily discouraged unless it can be backed up by clear-cut evidence, James Watson and Francis Crick's published findings regarding DNA structure engaged in speculations that led scientists to make their seminal discovery. If the two scientists had not added a paragraph stating their suspicions, they may have delayed the scientific community's recognition that DNA is genetic material.

When writing a seven-page formal lab report for my introductory chemistry laboratory course during my first year at the University of Virginia, I had to omit mention of integral stages of my reasoning. I had been given a checklist with forty-five items to complete; throughout the rubric, the most common requirement was "uses ACS (American Chemical Society) formatting," which meant that I had to scan through dense online texts filled with many rules and even more exceptions to those rules. Despite forcing myself to read and annotate the ACS manual, I was still penalized in my procedure section because my grader commented that "there was too much unnecessary narration in my procedure." Although the grader stated that my procedure was too detailed, I believed some of the steps I included were necessary and beneficial for my understanding when conducting the experiment. After our professor received many complaints from students regarding the confusing ACS formatting, she insisted that, if we ever wanted to become involved in scientific academia, we had to become used to the tedious rules that must be followed in order for our findings to be published. In my other post-lab reports for that class, there was a section in the rubric dedicated entirely to grammar. To receive full points in this category, you had to go "above expectations for grammar," though grammatical expectations were never clarified.

As I completed more lab courses and wrote more reports, I began resenting the need to write about my scientific discoveries, even when I was excited about my findings. I despised the thought of fitting my data into a certain framework by withdrawing all emotion and excitement from the accounts of my scientific discoveries. Due to these experiences in science classes, I came to associate writing with boring, dense, and unnecessary guidelines that dulled the articulations of my insights. The experiments themselves, by contrast, were filled with excitement and curiosity; they were an outlet for my creative ideas. And yet, I believed that to write for science meant to write without passion or voice.

My experiences with science writing are not limited to one rigid chemistry professor. The strict expectations for STEM writing have been continuously discussed and debated within the scientific community. For example, narration is discouraged, as this approach supposedly interferes with the delineation of a paper's findings. For example, the authors of the *Survival Guide to Academic Writing*, published by the University of Western Australia, instruct young scientists to "Avoid expressing personal judgment" and "Avoid emotive language" (UWA 1). I understand that when a scientist reports his or her findings, clarity is paramount, but I do not agree with the notion that the slightest addition of narration or emotion will impede such clarity. Furthermore, I believe that allowing scientists to integrate creativity into their scientific findings will make the paper more rewarding for both the writer and reader.

Scientists have long complained about editors' immediate dismissal of any form of creativity in communicating their results. For example, Stephen Heard, an ecologist at University of New Brunswick, incorporated an analogy to clearly describe the mechanistic transfer of pollen between plants, stating that "there is considerable evidence for pollen transfer among florets by wind or shaking." He then supported the point by citing "Hall et al. 1957" as a reference to the songwriters of the Jerry Lee Lewis hit "Whole Lotta Shakin' Goin' On." The reviewer deleted the phrase in the publication, stating "'although I appreciated the levity of the reference, I think it is not appropriate for scientific publication'" (qtd. in Heard).

Heard counters with multiple examples in which scientists' use of narration clarify more abstract scientific concepts while echoing the joy they feel in making their discoveries. In fact, Charles Darwin incorporated narration into his groundbreaking publications regarding evolution and natural selection. In Darwin's conclusion to the *Origin of Species*, he states:

> There is grandeur in this view of life, with its several powers, having been originally breathed by the Creator into a few forms or into one; and that, whilst this planet has gone cycling on according to the fixed law of gravity, from so simple a beginning endless forms most beautiful and most wonderful have been, and are being, evolved.

In this paragraph, Darwin places his recent discovery of the evolution of species in the larger context of the creation of the universe. He clearly communicates the excitement and awe he feels regarding his discovery—which is justified, as he is now known as the father of modern biology.

And yet, over time, emotion and science have become divided. This phenomenon has been reinforced by the wildly popular myth of the right brain and left brain. This idea labels people who are more free-spirited and artistic as left-brained, while more logical and precise thinkers are right-brained. Though this myth has no scientific basis, it is very common for students to consider themselves one or the other. I once took this view of humanities and STEM, seeing them as opposites, incompatible enemies that worked against each other rather than together. This is the exact type of mindset at which I now scoff when my friends in STEM complain about their required writing classes, but I cannot deny that this very common perspective stems from the uncreative and bleak writing forced into science students.

How was I able to outgrow this mindset? Amid my newfound resentment towards writing, I was required to take a writing class my first semester of college. Due to a late enrollment time, I was placed in a class about fictional short stories, one I was not very interested in. Despite my initial wariness with the class, I found my creativity reaching new heights as I wrote several argumentative essays and short stories. I loved the explosion of ideas I experienced reading every short story and deciding which character or plot twist to make the focus of my essay. The writing process I was learning in the class was different from the cold, uncreative writing I learned in chemistry lab; my creativity and excitement with the short stories came through in every sentence I wrote. In my writing class, my penchant for bold, strange ideas, such as transforming my argumentative essay into a dialogue or a letter, was both encouraged and rewarded. That class taught me to not ice out the passion I have for my ideas but rather to make them the very essence and purpose of what I wrote, a philosophy I've carried with me outside of the classroom. By incorporating the originality and personality that Sand-Jensen mentions is broadly discouraged in scientific writing, I was counterintuitively able to land my first college scientific research assistant position.

Although I had sent out several formal emails to professors inquiring about an undergraduate research assistant position, I was met mostly with rejections or no-replies. Acquiring this position was important to me, since most medical schools strongly recommend that applicants participate in a laboratory research apprenticeship. With several hundred pre-medical students at UVA and a limited number of labs accepting undergraduate researchers, it was stressful trying to craft the perfect email to the principal investigator of each lab. The emails I initially sent out were detached, simply stating my research and career interests and asking for a position. After a few rejections, I tried a more personal account of inspirations for my interests in neurodegeneration and how my work in the lab would complement the work I hope to do in the future. Although this approach did result in a few rejections, it also landed me an acceptance into the lab in which I currently work, where I have been able to conduct research I love. By applying what I learned in my writing class, I found that integrating enthusiasm and passion into my life as a scientist was advantageous rather than detrimental. Furthermore, I have found I am not alone in yearning for a more open and creative approach to writing in the world of science. The graduate student I assist enjoys explaining her findings through intricate and colorful drawings, which established scientific journals would instantly reject, despite their informativeness and pleasant aesthetic.

Currently, I am studying neuroimmunology, specifically the interactions between the neurons in our nervous system and macrophages, the "soldiers" of our immune system. When I present my research to my lab-mates, I always personify the elements in my scientific findings; for example, I have described the process of "macrophages grabbing and eating toxic neurons." I find that when I paint a story with my science, my lab-mates, fascinated with the "gobbling macrophages," are more engaged. With the addition of descriptive images and rich figurative language, the author can enhance the purpose of the paper, which is to inform the readers of his or her novel scientific discovery.

Another argument championing figurative language in scientific writing comes from physicist Alan Lightman, who explains that the metaphor used by many physics professors comparing stars and galaxies as dots on the surface of an expanding balloon has "helped students in cosmology […] in every country and every language where the subject is taught." The use of metaphor as a pedagogical device to explain complex scientific concepts is essential to the process of scientific discovery. In fact, in Newton's diaries, there are entries comparing the nature of light to a moving tennis ball. The use of metaphors seems to have aided Newton in the process of deciphering the mechanisms of light. If figurative language and imagery aid scientists in their progress toward scientific discoveries, this language should be included in scientific writing to help the audience visualize the process of discovery—rather than being dismissed as "flowery language" and completely omitted. Both my personal experiences and the works of prominent scientists support the incorporation of the forms of creativity that are often involved in scientists' own understanding of their research into the scientific writing process. Narration can provide readers with clarity about the scientific process since they are able to imagine it from the point of view of the scientist.

However, silencing a scientist's voice is not the only issue presented by rigid scientific writing conventions. Close analysis of these conventions shows that there is a strict preference for Western scientific English; they do not accommodate international scientists who may not be familiar with these set guidelines. Mooney and Evans discuss the concept of "Global Englishes," referring to the multiple Englishes around the world, such as Singlish, Indian English, and pidgin English. Kachru further details the circles of English with an inner circle, outer circle, and expanding circle. The inner circle represents Englishes such as the UK, USA, and Australia which provide the norms, while the outer circles are norm-dependent since they do not have cultural permission to change the norms set in place. According to Mooney and Evans, there are two responses to the presented World Englishes: the English-as-the-lingua-franca model, in which students are instructed in Standard English and value local varieties less than standard varieties, and the World Englishes model, which values all local English varieties with none marked as deficient (Mooney and Evans). Currently, scientific writing follows the first approach, using Western English as the lingua franca, with all top fifty scientific journals publishing in English from the U.S. or U.K. In addition, around 80% of all scientific journals are published in English.

I hypothesize that the lack of diversity within scientific writing organizations is what has led to the linguistic domination of Western English in scientific discourse. Though scientific academia emphasizes the need for unbiased and data-driven research, they fail to apply the same principles in understanding the need for diversity within scientific writing publications. When asked by *The New York Times*, major journals such as *Cell, eLife, Jama Network, the Lancet, PLOS, PNAS, the New England Journal of Medicine* and *Springer Nature* were unable to provide data on racial and ethnic diversity of researchers published on their platforms. Only the *American Association for the Advancement of Science* and *Royal Society* were able to provide data on authors and reviewers, though the data only accounted for ten to twenty percent of recent authors, thus rendering any conclusions or data analysis of diversity unreliable.

Though many journals fail to collect data on the scientists they publish, they do have data, though unpromising, on the racial and ethnic diversity of employees involved in the publication process. Close to 90% of the members of the *Royal Society*'s editorial boards are white. Among editors employed in the United States by *PLOS*, 74% are white; none identify as Black. Roughly 80% of *A.A.A.S.* leadership, including editors and advisers, are white. In addition, the entire leadership team of *eLife* is white, and there are no Black editors for *Cell*. With a serious lack of diversity within scientific writing leadership, it is clear how the English-as-the-*lingua-franca* model has flourished in the scientific community.

Scientific academia largely ignores the relevance of its lack of racial and ethnic diversity to the rigid requirements of scientific writing. Healthy science in the academy requires scientists ranging in gender, race, ethnicity, disability, and sexuality, and more. These factors are essential for the advancement of knowledge, since scientists can collaborate with communities often ignored and/or exploited by previous or present discriminatory practices of Western scientists. Thus, it is essential to ensure that the scientific writing community provides more resources to raise the confidence and therefore the contributions of scientists who may not be familiar or comfortable with Western scientific writing guidelines. Until there is more established change within scientific journals regarding the required formatting, it is critical that we work to increase comfort and familiarity with the current scientific writing guidelines. Without proper guidance for researchers to navigate the often-strange world of scientific writing, many creative researchers are rejected, and many novel scientific ideas are wasted.

When I spoke to my father about his experience as an international student, he echoed many of the same concerns, detailing his experiences in a graduate program. After graduating with a physics degree from a small college in India, he came to America to continue graduate school, he told me he found himself "falling behind on [his] research because no one would clarify when [he] was confused." Specifically, he found that his supervisors often deemed him lazy, that he "used trivial language and made grammatical errors in his scientific writing," rather than understanding that these issues resulted from his struggle to use English as his primary scientific language, something he had never done before. He also told me how he was often fearful about presenting his research because he was scared how faculty would respond to his grammar and his accent. Dealing with many racist encounters at his small Midwestern college campus in the 1990s, he became more reserved, hoping to avoid the harassment he often dealt with due to his accent. Although he was and continues to be passionate about physics, he decided to take a more industrial job rather than one in academia, partly due to the discouragement he faced from his peers and educators. His accent and his inability to immediately adjust to scientific writing guidelines prevented him from pursuing a career that he'd traveled halfway around the world to achieve.

My father's story is not an isolated incident. A study of international graduate students highlights language barriers, difficulty accessing research resources, and differences in educational and cultural background as main areas of difficulty that these students face. International students often mention their lack of knowledge about the rules and regulations of ethical research and referencing as a barrier to their work. In several Asian countries, there are very limited guidelines on ethical standards, especially regarding human subjects, often requiring little to no review. In addition, several Chinese students in the study found the concept of plagiarism hard to grasp since referencing is considered optional, rather than a requirement, in many Chinese research areas. Students emphasized the difficulty of adjusting to American thesis writing, which they categorized as a highly tedious task. The common solution to these struggles in their home countries is to rely on their supervisors. However, scientific graduate school in America often requires its students to learn independently, especially when it comes to tasks that are considered "self-explanatory," such as writing.

Evans and Mooney mention that "until negative attitudes to outer and expanding varieties of English change, a local variety of English will not be as valuable as standard English" (236). In the scientific writing field, in which writing guidelines sidelining World Englishes have remained constant for several decades, it is essential we provide additional resources for the teaching of science writing. The solution I propose is the creation of scientific writing centers to serve as resources for student researchers, helping them feel more comfortable and confident in writing and presenting their work.

Elisabeth Heseltine, a science editor who has worked in many major publishing journals including *Cell*, has discussed how there are no suitable workshops that teach the structure and formation of scientific papers for researchers whose first language is not English. She insists that it is vital that this skill of structuring scientific papers be taught as a subject in its own right, arguing that it should be considered an essential part of general training in research (Heseltine). With the creation of a science writing center satellite, this vital step in the scientific process can finally be acknowledged and discussed by both the pedagogy and science communities.

Many research universities receive more than 1.5 billion dollars in proposal activity and 500 million dollars in awards annually. For effective collaboration between administrative faculty, research scientists, and financial administrators, a clear and succinct line of communication is required. This communication often takes the form of grant proposals, abstracts, and project presentations. Consequently, it is vital that the university provides extensive resources and guidance to all research faculty and students—to ensure that the many established scientific writing guidelines do not hinder this innovative, creative research taking place.

The primary goals of many research institutions such as UVA are to support faculty, improve accountability, and generate opportunities. The creation of science-centered writing centers would advance these goals. Not only would it improve the generation of research at UVA, but it would also vastly improve the quality of the scientists that emerge from UVA's research programs.

In sum, I propose, first, the creation of a science writing satellite with specialist tutors extensively trained in the conventions of lab reports (formal records of conducted experiments, including objectives, procedures, and results); research proposals (documents explaining what students plan to research, why it's worth researching, and research methodology); research presentations (visual versions of research papers that allow researchers to obtain feedback); manuscripts (write-ups of research intended for publication); and abstracts (concise overviews of scientific research processes that provide a general understanding of the research).

One study found that tutors without disciplinary expertise struggled to help writers see "the larger, more global problems with their drafts" (Wang et al.). Specialist tutors, who have knowledge regarding the genre of the paper because they have either taken courses in that specific field or have been specifically trained to tutor in it, could alleviate that problem. A tutor with a general understanding of scientific writing requirements can more efficiently assess why their tutee may have not received full points on his or her assignment. Such tutors are also more likely to be familiar with the formatting guidelines that are commonly used in university science courses, including ACS Style (chemistry research), Springer Journal Formatting (Springer Interdisciplinary Journal), and Purdue Owl Engineering Paper (physics research). Considering the wide range of universities and scientific fields, these writing centers should also closely monitor shifts in required scientific writing formatting, in order to keep tutors up to date. It would also be beneficial to recruit students who have already completed STEM courses or to encourage these students to collaborate with tutors to give input on techniques the students have utilized to improve their own scientific writing.

Second, I also propose that writing center tutors and administrations create an easy-to-read scientific writing guide for general distribution. Many colleges have already formed scientific writing guides directed towards researchers on their campuses. A scientific writing guide can be an efficient resource for researchers who want to ensure that their work generally follows the conventions of the genres. It can also encourage researchers to take scientific writing guidelines more into consideration when writing, as well as to seek help from their local writing center.

Third, I propose that writing center tutors and administrators collaborate with researchers to set up pop-up scientific writing workshops in different labs across campuses. Every research lab has weekly or bi-weekly lab meetings for the discussion of common research topics or general improvements that the lab can make. During this time, writing center administrators can set up a presentation to talk about the relevance of scientific writing and to discuss the available resources with which researchers can improve their scientific writing.

Dr. Anna Clemens, an academic writing coach who has taught researchers at various universities including Imperial College London and Czech Academy of Sciences, emphasizes the need for scientific training workshops to lessen researchers' fear of rejection from high-impact journals. She mentions that the common theme she encounters among her several hundred clients is that they almost always have great scientific research but are often rejected from high-ranking journals due to their inability to write for the wider scientific writing community. An implementation of a scientific writing workshop could challenge scientists to collectively shift their focus onto how to communicate their labs' research more effectively.

Fourth, I propose training scientific supervisors to support editing scientific papers and presentations. Due to their lack of training in scientific writing pedagogy, many supervisors are ambivalent about working on papers with their graduate students. In a study, several supervisors indicated that they "refused to help students with basic English skills" (Wang et al.). Indeed, they indicated that they didn't see developing those skills as part of their jobs, suggesting that it was, instead, a task for English lecturers. In the same study, many graduate students said that a lack of supervisor expertise in teaching writing and/or English was a major problem when developing drafts of their thesis. Providing training for the professionals working closest to research students can create a more direct pipeline of communication that is more easily accessible to research students.

Many colleges explore the intersection of creativity and STEM. For instance, many universities feature the Art of Science programs; materials scientist Dante Zakhidov hosted an exhibition at Stanford University, the purpose of which was to show that "thinking creatively is something that pertains to all fields" (Taylor); and the Poets for Science exhibition encourages scientists to demonstrate the connection between poetry and particular areas of science. Similar exhibitions could encourage scientists to not completely suppress their voices and passions when communicating their research.

Finally, I propose that writing centers collaborate with scientists to hold symposia or workshops that encourage scientific creativity and the incorporation of one's own dialect into one's research. The purpose of these workshops would be to help scientists integrate their passion for their research into writing or other creative outlets. Considering my suffocating experiences I felt within the restrictive scientific writing guidelines, I believe that workshops encouraging scientific creativity and the incorporation of one's own dialect could shift the attitude of scientists towards writing, alleviating some of the fear and anxiety often associated with scientific communication. Workshops and symposia, even when they are not officially associated with scientific journals, can encourage scientists to be more confident and open with ideas and findings. Scientists from different cultural backgrounds could be encouraged to express their findings however they choose, communicating with their audiences in the languages and registers that best suit their discoveries.

Works Cited

Britannica, The Editors of Encyclopedia. "Are There Really Right-Brained and Left-Brained People?". *Encyclopedia Britannica*, 23 May 2017, https://www.britannica.com/story/are-there-really-right-brained-and-left-brained-people. Accessed 4 January 2024.

Clemmons, Anna. "Research Writers Academy." Dr. Anna Clemmons, https://www.annaclemens.com/about. Accessed 21 January 2024.

Heard, Stephen. "On Whimsy, Jokes, and Beauty: Can Scientific Writing Be Enjoyed?" *Ideas in Ecology and Evolution*, vol. 7, no. 1, 2014, https://doi.org/10.4033/iee.2014.7.14.f.

Elisabeth Heseltine. "Teaching Scientific Writing to Non-

Native English Speakers, Medical Writing," 22:1, 13-16, 2013, DOI: 10.1179/204748012X13560931063591

Huttner-Koros, Adam. "Why Science's Universal Language Is a Problem for Research." *The Atlantic*, Atlantic Media Company, 14 Sept. 2015, Huttner-Koros, Adam. www.theatlantic.com/science/archive/2015/08/english-universal-language-science-research/400919/.

Ianetta, Melissa, and Lauren Fitzgerald. *The Oxford Guide for Writing Tutors: Practice and Research*. Oxford University Press, 2016.

Lightman, Alan P. "SCIENCE: Magic on the Mind Physicists' Use of Metaphor." *The American Scholar*, vol. 58, no. 1, 1989, pp. 97–101, www.jstor.org/stable/41211647.

Mooney, Annabelle, and Betsy Evans. *Language, Society and Power*. Routledge, 20 Feb. 2015. https://doi.org/10.4324/9781315733524.

Research UVA. University of Virginia, 2024, https://info.researchuva.virginia.edu/. Accessed 4 Jan. 2024

Sand-Jensen, Kaj. "How to Write Consistently Boring Scientific Literature." *Oikos*, vol. 116, no. 5, 2007, pp. 723–727., https://doi.org/10.1111/j.0030-1299.2007.15674.x.

Sawir, Erlenawati. "Language Difficulties of International Students in Australia: The Effects of Prior Learning Experience." *International Education Journal*, vol. 6, no. 5, 2005, pp. 567–580, files.eric.ed.gov/fulltext/EJ855010.pdf. Accessed 4 Jan. 2024.

Singh, Amarjeet & Singh, Harkomal & Chanotra, Rajjat & Doreen, Ihogoza & AW, Taylor-Robinson & Kumar, Bimlesh. "Knowledge, attitude and practices of university pharmacy students and academic professionals towards scientific writing: a questionnaire-based study." *Journal of Hospital Pharmacy*. 2017, pp 200-216. https://www.researchgate.net/publication/320272221_Knowledge_attitude_and_practices_of_university_pharmacy_students_and_academic_professionals_towards_scientific_writing_a_questionnaire-based_study

Survival Guide Academic Writing Style: Objectivity. www.uwa.edu.au/students/-/media/Project/UWA/UWA/Students/Docs/STUDYSmarter/GE11-Academic-Writing-Style_Objectivity.pdf.

Taylor, Carly. "Creative Reencounters with Research in Art of Science 2020 Exhibition." *The Stanford Daily*, 15 June 2020, https://www.stanforddaily.com/2020/06/11/creative-reencounters-with-research-in-art-of-science-2020-exhibition/.

Wang, I.-C., J. N. Ahn, H. J. Kim, and X. Lin-Siegler. "Why Do International Students Avoid Communicating with Americans?" *Journal of International Students*, vol. 7, no. 3, July 2018, pp. 555-82, doi:10.32674/jis.v7i3.288.

9 Finding Power in Marginalization: Preserving Nurture in the Writing Center

Kaitlyn Baker

Abstract

This paper seeks to understand the ways in which university writing centers have become feminized due to their association with nurturing and emotional labor. In response to critics who have suggested deemphasizing these features to obtain greater institutional respect, this paper argues that writing center directors should reject assimilationism and foster sites of radical nurture. By asserting their own power, writing centers can claim the value of 'women's work' and serve as examples of the potency and necessity of emotional labor. The paper concludes with suggestions for how writing centers might structure themselves as feminist spaces.

Introduction

When entering the writing center at the University of Virginia, one immediately notices its nurturing environment. The plush sofas, house plants, and coffee stations clearly communicate that this is a space meant to be comfortable. The tutors inside, bending over writers' work, are predominantly female-presenting. The space seems different from the typical lecture hall, wherein students remain seated in rows as a lone lecturer assumes authority over the room, dominating the space and creating a hierarchical relationship between professor and students. Indeed, some writing center scholars have taken note of the peculiar interplay between the nurturing environment typical in writing centers and their largely female staffs; they have observed, in other words, the feminization of the writing center. To be feminized is to "be disempowered within the patriarchy, to be the object of systematic oppression," but the writing center is also feminized because of its adoption of feminist principles (Traschel 26). The writing center incorporates collaboration and nurturing, features that distinguish it from the broader academy. In this paper, I will draw on the work of writing center scholars and feminist theorists, placing the writing center in the context of feminist discourse. I will further the argument that the writing center has become a niche, feminized space within the university—and therefore can serve as a "homeplace" of resistance. Furthermore, by embracing feminist theory, writing center scholars can claim nurture as an intellectual choice and affirm the value of emotional labor within the academy.

Feminist Principles Within the Writing Center

Though feminist theory as a mode of intellectual inquiry is diverse, one can identify certain similarities among most feminist work. Feminist theorist and Montana State University Writing Center Director Michelle Miley defines feminist theory as "a set of long-established practices that advocates a political position for rights and responsibilities that certainly include the equality of women and others [...] embodying the feminist principles of equality, respect, and coalition building" (49). These feminist principles are reflected in the work of writing centers, which operate by pairing writers with peer tutors. In comparison to the relationship between a professor or a graduate teaching assistant and a student, the tutor-client relationship involves relative equals. *The Oxford Guide for Writing Tutors,* a comprehensive and seminal work used to prepare and train tutors, defines the tutor-client relationship separately from the teacher-student relationship. The guide states that, "in a Writing Center, success is determined by an agenda negotiated by the tutor and writer, and often its primary assessment of success is conducted by the writer herself" (Fitzgerald and Ianetta 18). This negotiation allows the client a significant degree of power. The client decides which materials to consider during a session, as well as which topics within those materials to center in the conversation. Ultimately, in the writing center, both client and tutor must respect the needs and wishes of the other. An ideal tutorial is akin to a conversation between equal parties. This rejection of traditional academic hierarchies is typical in both writing center pedagogy and feminist practices. Meg Woolbright notes that "both feminist and writing center commentators advocate teaching methods that are non-hierarchical, cooperative, interactive ventures between students and tutors talking about issues grounded in the students' own experience" (18). Woolbright contrasts the feminist writing center with the patriarchal academy that insists on clear, hierarchical divisions between student and instructor.

Despite this close association, writing center scholars have been hesitant to fully embrace feminist theory. In "Bringing Feminist Theory Home," Miley demonstrates that, while scholars recognize feminist principles within their work and within the Center, there are not "many scholars claiming feminist theory as the primary theory through which they mediate their work" (52). To understand this phenomenon, it is important to regard writing center faculty as disciples of the academy. Despite their supposed stances of dissent or resistance with respect to the patriarchal academy, many such faculty were trained in its practices. Indeed, in describing the opposition between "female" and "male" forms of rhetoric, Thomas Farrell reminds his readers that "since the male mode of argumentation is taught in schools and colleges, it is not surprising to find many women who write and speak in the male mode" (1). The male form of rhetoric is passed along as an academic tradition, despite evidence that the female mode of rhetoric might invoke deeper thought and consideration by the reader, and despite evidence that embracing female modes of rhetoric may allow more female students to express their thoughts more easily (Nichols 590).

Farrell identifies these two forms of rhetoric, but he does not challenge them, insisting that the male form of rhetoric should be privileged over the female form. His writings are useful as proof that collaborative writing and feminist pedagogy are in fact marginalized within the academy, a circumstance which can cause some proponents of such pedagogies—ones with less support or privilege—to confront institutional consequences. Faced with the choice between two forms of rhetoric, one of which is associated with the marginalized sex, in the context of an academy in which, at all levels, expression in that marginalized form of rhetoric is slighted, many women who are seeking to gain more institutional respect will embrace the dominant form and eschew the other. In addition, writing centers and Women's Studies programs developed at the same time but independently, with both fledgling programs seeking to gain a footing within the academy—thereby compounding the effects of marginalization.

Whatever has contributed to the lack of discourse between writing center scholarship and feminist theory, it may be difficult to overcome. To participate in feminist pedagogy, writing center faculty must make the conscious, difficult choice to resist the dominant mores of the academy. Some scholars have suggested that the collaborative work of writing centers requires some skepticism towards institutions, which separates the work of the writing center from that of the broader academy. In considering how a feminist model of tutoring may impact the writing center, Jean Marie Lutes suggests that "the ethic of collaboration and a skepticism towards established authorities" form the very basis of feminist tutoring (248). In order both to participate in feminist pedagogy and to exist within the academy, those contributing to writing centers should fully embrace the strength of their pedagogy, even—or especially—as it stands in opposition to the broader academy.

The Feminization of the Writing Center

Because it embodies feminist teaching, the writing center is distinct from the broader academy—and this separation comes with institutional consequences. One reason writing centers are marginalized within the academy is their association with nurture and emotional labor. In "Nurturant Ethics and Academic Ideals: Convergence in the Writing Center," Mary Trachsel describes how her dual roles as a mother and a director of a writing center interact. In her journey to reconcile those roles, Trachsel discovered that she had to deconstruct "boundaries I had either discovered or erected between the concepts of 'work' and 'not-work'" (25). Conventionally, 'work' is construed as authoring, producing, and teaching, while 'not-work' is construed as collaborating, discussing, and nurturing.

The academy depends on this masculinized, individualistic conception of work. This emphasis surfaces in the academy's strict protections against plagiarism, which would harm the scholar's property claims over his work. In fact, those who embrace the individualistic view of scholarship receive better wages and institutional positions. By contrast, the writing center presents a feminist approach to learning. During a session, tutors learn to "build rapport, to motivate students, and to give helpful feedback, without, however, resorting to any feedback that might make the students feel criticized or judged" (Nelson et al. 164). To meet these expectations, writing centers recruit tutors who are the "nurturing type" (Trachsel 27). This means that they seek out students who are highly empathetic, those who would give a friendly face to the writing center as an institution and, by proxy, to the act of composition more generally. The skills required to be a successful writing tutor, including "empathy, patience, sensitivity, diplomacy, friendliness," are coded feminine. The distinct nurturing approach of composition programs and writing centers feminizes the programs, placing them and those that labor within them firmly in the category of 'not work.'

Associated with caregiving, writing centers assume the challenges of 'women's work,' including lower funding and a more tenuous position within the academy. However, perhaps the most pernicious consequence of the association between the writing center and feminized labor is the denial of writing centers scholars' intellectual credit. Traschel writes that "feminine identity [...] is excluded from the realm of academic endeavor because of its association with emotional attachment and interpersonal connectedness" (27). Writing center directors and scholars, including when they are well respected within the field of Composition Studies or even granted tenure, are marginalized. In "Rearticulating the Work of the Writing Center," Nancy Grimm tells the story of a friend who was nominated for a prestigious teaching award. Beside her name on the posted list of nominated teachers, Grimm's friend noticed that a colleague had drawn question marks (Grimm 523-4). Even when nominated for prestigious awards, the work of writing center scholars is disregarded due to its association with emotional labor.

The writing center is also hindered by its reputation as a 'fix-it shop,' a place where students may go for basic grammatical instruction and quick fixes. Instead of being treated as scholars, writing center faculty are sometimes regarded merely as "remedial teachers begging for respectability" (North 433). Indeed, this misconception is so pernicious that writing centers must overtly address the issue in mission statements and interviews. On its homepage, the Writing Center at the University of Virginia reminds its clients that tutors will not "'fix' your paper for you," nor will tutors "proofread or edit for you." Likewise, the Writing Center Director at Villanova University remarked in an interview that "the largest misconception about the writing center is that we are a 'fix-it' shop, simply here to mark grammar and punctuation errors, and then send the writer on his merry way" (Flood 1). The website for the Writing Center at the University of North Texas similarly laments that "students and faculty alike tend to think of the center as a place limited to remediation because there is not a clear understanding of tutorial instruction and methodology that is implemented in these centers" (Writing Center Philosophy). The sheer pervasiveness of these disclaimers proves that there is broad misunderstanding of the philosophies and scholarship that undergird writing center work. Professors who send students to the writing center to launder their papers fundamentally misunderstand the work of the center, and, in doing so, remain ignorant to the rich body of writing center scholarship.

This version of work and scholarship that depends heavily on emotional labor exists in opposition to the academy, but it is also a creation of the academy. Indeed, the nurturing approach used by tutors and directors is a direct response to "the challenging (and often less than clear) demands of academic writing" (Nelson et al. 165). The impersonal nature of the typical classroom environment does not allow the student to collaborate with his or her instructor to resolve unanswered questions. Even sympathetic instructors may not be experienced in emotional labor and nurture. To support students struggling to learn from and with such instructors, the writing center aspires towards the "development of an atmosphere of mutual respect, trust, and community; shared leadership; a cooperative structure; the integration of cognitive and affective learning; and action" (Woolbright 17). The approach assumed by writing center faculty conflicts with but also buttresses the typical classroom environment. Pedagogically, the writing center is integral but set apart.

The physical landscape of the writing center also contributes to its separation from the other academic spaces that surround it. Perhaps because of this marginalization, writing centers seek to create comfortable environments. Aspects of the physical space are intended to echo the collaborative and nurturing environment of the center. When describing their space, writing center faculty often used descriptive words like "soft, calming, welcoming, comfortable, familiar, non-threatening, and friendly" (McKinney 8). It is not coincidental that the physical aspects of the space mimic the qualities of the ideal tutor who occupies it. Jackie McKinney argues that female writing center faculty constructed writing center environments in this way to create a "female space in opposition to the institution at large, which was male, uncomfortable, foreign" (17). It is difficult to state with certainty whether the feminization of writing centers occurred because a predominantly female staff created feminine environments or because the clients called for emotional labor, which attracted female staff. However, regardless of the reasons, the characteristics of the writing center serve to separate it from the broader academy. McKinney writes that "having couches or photos or coffee pots is an effort to construct a space different from classrooms and other impersonal institutional spaces" (7). This environment signals an unconventional approach to learning, one involving nurturing and collaboration. It is meant to assuage the feelings of anxiety students may associate with writing. Implicit in this environment is also a critique of typical classrooms that demand professionalism and individualism. Because it offers a different vision of a learning environment, the physical landscape of the writing center resists the patriarchal academy.

Some scholars have viewed these developments with alarm, believing that it is necessary to resist the gendering, and subsequent marginalization, of writing center spaces. These scholars suggest that the writing center should assimilate within the academy. McKinney suggests that "female directors who insist on cozy, inviting spaces may be unwittingly narrating their work as nonintellectual in the eyes of some" (17). However, assimilation would require the abandonment of the nurturing approach, which provides many pedagogical benefits for writing center faculty. Since the feminization of the writing center depends on its association with emotional labor, one cannot un-gender the space without abandoning those nurturing qualities. Critics therefore seek to downplay the nurturing characteristics which make writing centers the "handmaidens of autonomous literacy" (Grimm 524). Critics attempt to "redefine the work performed in writing centers as something more intellectually rigorous and respectable" (Trachsel 31). Un-gendering the space would involve fashioning the writing center as a typical classroom environment and reinstating the hierarchical teacher-student relationship. It would thus involve a shift away from nurturing and feminist principles.

Writing Centers as Homeplaces

It is crucial that writing centers maintain their emphasis on care and collaboration because they provide a space for nurture not found elsewhere in an increasingly Fordist university system. In "Labor Pains: A Political Analysis of Writing Center Tutoring," Linda Shamoon and Deborah Burns liken modern universities to assembly lines that produce academics and professionals. Using a Neo-Marxist framework, Shamoon and Burns describe how industrialization has led universities to incorporate Fordist systems. Modern universities are concerned with "the breaking apart of complex tasks into their simplest units of work in order to make possible large-scale production of easily reproducible parts, and the creation of easily filled slots for labor" (63). Students and faculty often experience the Fordist strains of university life when they are shoved into increasingly large classes, some of which are made possible using unpaid or low-paid teaching assistants and adjuncts.

Students are positioned as units of production moving through the university; by the completion of their tenures, they will become products of the university. They will be representatives of the advantages of a university education, and employers will be able to verify their skills and knowledge via diplomas. However, while they are still working towards completion, these students are also resources that provide prestige and money to the university. For the student, this experience can be one of impersonality and alienation. Because, as a Fordist institution, the university has an interest in maximizing productivity and minimizing costs, students are often unable to form personal relationships with their instructors and have little access to collaborative or nurturing education.

Within the Fordist institution, the writing center occupies a unique position. Because it is set apart from the rest of the university as a space of emotional labor, it can become a platform for resistance. The writing center can provide personal, specialized experiences for students, experiences based on nurturing unlikely to be found in classrooms. The feminist principles already present in the writing center—those of collaboration, equality, and respect—place the writing center in opposition to the Fordist institution. In contrast to the "assembly-line" model of the Fordist academy, the writing center becomes what bell hooks calls a "homeplace." In her essay "Homeplace (a site of resistance)," hooks describes how Black women construct their homeplaces as refuges from the racism they face in the outside environments; in doing so, she provides a useful model for interpreting writing centers as sites of resistance. Homeplaces provide Black women with the "opportunity to grow and develop, to nurture our spirits" (384). hooks acknowledges that sexism has led to this task being delegated to Black women, but she also states that "it does not matter" (385). The task of creating caring spaces is so vital that it is more important to maintain than to eschew them because they represent histories of oppression.

While the experiences within the writing center are not comparable to the experiences of Black women evading violent racism, hooks provides a useful framework for considering the position of the writing center within an academic institution. The center is marginalized because of sexism, and it is tempting to abandon nurture to gain more respect. However, "it does not matter" (385) because the collective task of resisting the Fordist institution is far more important than individual desires for institutional esteem. Furthermore, hooks writes that the homeplace has been "a crucial site for organizing, for forming political solidarity. Homeplace has been a site of resistance" (388). The writing center has the unique opportunity to become a site of resistance not despite its feminization, but because of it. If the writing center can utilize this separation effectively, it can become an embodied critique of the Fordist university—an alternative model of education that does not involve the standardization of students and faculty.

Writing centers can find power in this oppositional stance. In *Bitter Milk*, Madeleine Grumet writes that recovering feminist thought in a masculinized education system "is the task of recognizing unity in what we see as separate, the task of claiming exemption, as well, from the universal law and claiming separateness despite the wish for unity" (191). Claiming power involves accepting the writing center's separation and determining how it can be used for further resistance. It also involves fully incorporating (and claiming) feminist theory within the writing center. In "Feminist Mothering: A Theory/Practice for Writing Center Administration," Michelle Miley asks, "could the caregiving work of writing centers, caregiving Traschel ties to our roots, be vitally necessary in university systems where students often experience intense stress to keep up with the pace of capitalistic production?" (18). To answer this question, Miley draws on the work of feminist theorist Andrea O'Reilly. In her work *Feminist Mothering*, Andrea O'Reilly defines mothering or providing care as political and activist work. In the chapter "This is What Feminism Is," she explains how mothering can exist separately from the patriarchal institution of motherhood. In other words, O'Reilly is concerned with how nurturing can continue even when it is punished by patriarchal institutions. In response to such punishment, she calls for mothering to become a "site, role, and identity of power for women '' (193). Joan Tronto expands ethics of care to relational interactions beyond the mother-child relationship. She portrays "neediness as ontologically basic to human function" (qtd. in Trachsel 35). By recognizing that students benefit from care, writing centers can fulfill a niche within the academy and transform feminization narratives into narratives of power.

Embracing a Feminist Writing Center

Because the writing center can use its status as a separate entity to the advantage of its clients, separation can be a source of power. As such, it is not wise to abandon the writing center's nurturing approach. In fact, to fully realize its niche role, the writing center should analyze the ways in which assimilationist tendencies have infiltrated its pedagogy. Michelle Miley hypothesizes that such tendencies, including the desire to avoid casting writing centers as "domesticated, feminized spaces," reflect "the feelings of degradation" shared by many of the faculty and staff working at writing centers (19). In a survey of writing center directors, Dave Healy found that, overwhelmingly, his subjects reported "being under-resourced, underpaid, untenured, and undervalued" (Healy 38). Choosing resistance can be difficult when it means difficulty obtaining funding and respect, and it can be even more difficult when one considers that writing centers often are forced to justify their existence in onerous assessments. However, if the writing center yields to the predominant narrative associated with feminization—that to be feminized is to "be disempowered within the patriarchy, to be the object of systematic oppression" (Trachsel 26)—then it ignores and rejects the power associated with its separation from the academy.

Furthermore, in portraying traditional (masculinized) scholarship as the norm to which the writing center must adhere, assimilationist scholars deny the intellectual value of its work. Mary Traschel articulates this very position when she writes, "by choosing to view 'women's work'"—in this case, writing center work— "from the ideological perspective of the fathers, we are complicitous in its devaluation" (34). In other words, part of the writing center's mission should be to challenge the basic assumptions undergirding its marginalization. Shifting the focus away from nurturing work concedes that emotional labor is inferior. In attempting to align the writing center with the 'work' of the academy, these critics imply that its current and previous activities, as stated before, are 'not work.' Beyond the academy, this viewpoint also upholds the devaluation of women's work and undermines feminist principles. By contrast, the positioning of the writing center as separate allows it to radically assert the power of feminist nurture.

To resolve the problems associated with the feminization narrative, the writing center must assert the intellectual value of emotional labor, despite the marginalization such labor could bring. The writing center must claim nurturing as an intellectual choice and situate it as a "disciplined and academically rigorous pedagogy" (Trachsel 35). In "The Uses of the Margins," Lil Brannon and Steven North affirm the writing center's continuous struggle towards "viability," but they insist that it can find viability only by exploiting its "marginal position" and creating "a rhetoric of marginality that will use [its] status for institutional advantage" (North 10). Writing center scholars can use their marginalized positions to explore radical ideas, but they are also able to use their positions within the academy to share those ideas.

Furthermore, through scholarship, scholars can assert the value of the writing center. For example, in her work, Mary Traschel draws on human development theories to insist that nurturing provides authorship to both tutor and client. She quotes psychoanalyst Jessica Benjamin, who writes, "'a person comes to feel that 'I am the doer who does. I am the author of my acts,' by being with another person who recognizes her acts, her feelings, her intentions, her existence, her independence'" (qtd, in Traschel 37). By reinterpreting nurturing as an intellectual choice, Traschel claims its value without abandoning feminist principles. Trachsel creatively deploys psychological evidence to share the value of her pedagogical choices with her audience. She is an example of a scholar using her position to share the virtues of collaborative pedagogy.

Finally, the feminist writing center must be willing to engage with politics, especially racial politics; feminist theory is activist scholarship. Some scholars, like McKinney, have doubted the extent to which writing centers are comfortable spaces, wondering if they reflect instead a "certain class (upper or middle) and cultural background (white American)" (16). Case studies support this interpretation. Some scholars recount experiences in writing centers that speak both to their potential for radical politics and to the ways in which, inevitably, oppressive dynamics from outside those spaces enter them nonetheless. For example, in "Writing Center as Homeplace (A Site for Radical Resistance)," Kaidan McNamee, a nonbinary transmasculine person, writes, "I realized in short order that I was not only in a place where my transness was acceptable—it was a place where my transness was *valuable*. I saw and understood things that other tutors didn't; I was often challenged in a way that they weren't" (McNamee and Miley). However, his comfort would be shattered during experiences with clients who discounted his identity and the value of diversity. He describes one experience where a client, assuming that he was a cisgender individual, complained about "diversity quotas" (McNamee and Miley). In response, he was forced to disclose his status as a trans individual and spent the rest of the session listening to his client's apologies and concerns. In sum, the client's biases forced McNamee to create a comfortable environment for them, while experiencing prejudice and the resulting discomfort.

In that same essay, Michelle Miley gives her own, broader perspective on diversity and power within the writing center. After attending a workshop, she noticed that:

> the facilitators of the workshop asserted that, because writing centers work with language, and because language is powerful, we have a responsibility to effect change in our institutions by actively working for inclusive language. The point hit home. We do work the language. It is powerful. And because of that, we have the responsibility to be activists.

Tutors need to be extensively trained to respond to moments of cultural tension that can lead to harm. Tutors must also be empowered to challenge prejudice within the institution. Occasionally, that may mean abandoning a stance of unequivocal nurture for more difficult forms of emotional labor, including disclosure of marginalized identities and the active attempt to challenge prejudice.

In "Dear Writing Centers: Black Women Speaking Silence into Language and Action," Talia Nanton and Talisha Morrison challenge the idea of the writing center as "home," showing how important awareness of the power of language is in the writing center, particularly when it comes to race. Part of that piece is a manifesto that Nanton wrote, inspired by her experiences of racism within the writing center. In it, she rejects the notion of the writing center as a safe space, writing, "stop smiling in my face and acting like we're all friends and everything's cool, safe space bullshit, coworker I'm talking to you." Earlier in the piece, she describes other ways that the very determination of the writing center to be a safe space can manifest in racist policing of affect:

> As a Black woman, I was called "aggressive" by a peer and accused of "creating tension" and taking conversations "out of hand" when I stuck up for myself in debates where it seemed as though the opinions of others were welcome but not my own. I was reprimanded for being disrespectful after not saying "hello" to another co-worker, however unintentionally, all under the guise of making sure the center remained "a safe space." I was berated for the actions of other consultants, such as playing music too loud, and accused of not taking criticism well. (Nanton)

Such racism is a failure of the writing center to fully embody feminist principles and become a "homeplace." If feminist pedagogy does indeed revolve around the concepts of interaction, connectedness, nurture, and collaboration, racism constitutes an abject failure in the mission of the feminist writing center.

Aligning the writing center with nurture should not mean ignoring its status as a place where power and authority shape interactions. Writing center scholars should not shy away from conflict. Just as collaboration and nurture provide power to the writing center, "conflict and struggle are vital parts of revolutionary feminist pedagogy" (Buffington 10). In other words, nurture and conflict need not be mutually exclusive. Indeed, a crucial element of acknowledging the influence of emotional labor within the writing center is recognizing which groups are excluded from feeling at "home" in the space. To that end, Audrey Thompson writes:

> White, middle-class culture takes for granted the status of the home as a 'haven in a heartless world,' but historically, there has been no sure place of refuge for African Americans, since racism and poverty can invade any home. No home is altogether safe from the effects of low wages, and no home can prevent the burning of crosses on the front yard, invasion from lynch mobs, sexual harassment on the job, or joblessness due to racism. (523)

Only by engaging in this conflict and in radical politics can the feminist writing center repudiate colorblind theories of emotional labor and work towards creating a homeplace for all.

Conclusion: Rooms of Your Own

In "Professions for Women," Virginia Woolf writes:
> You have won rooms of your own in the house hitherto exclusively owned by men. You are able, though not without great labor and effort, to pay the rent. You are earning your five hundred pounds a year. But this freedom is only a beginning; the room is your own, but it is still bare. It has to be furnished; it has to be decorated; it has to be shared. How are you going to furnish it, how are you going to decorate it? With whom are you going to share it, and upon what terms? These, I think are questions of the utmost importance and interest. For the first time in history, you are able to ask them; for the first time you are able to decide for yourselves what the answers should be. (6)

Writing centers have organically developed as "rooms of [our] own." They have long used nurturing and comfortable spaces both as pedagogical tools and as attempts to set the center apart from the broader academy. Because of its separation, the writing center can be a site of radical resistance. It can provide an alternative, caring model for education based on collaboration, respect, and equality. Furthermore, the writing center can legitimize nurturing as a pedagogical tool. The feminist writing center must claim the value and power of 'women's work' but should also be careful to avoid structuring the center in such a way as to only represent white women. With this framework, writing centers can have far-reaching impacts on education, and writing center jobs can comprise much more than a "profession for women." Writing centers should openly claim their use of feminist theory, incorporating it into their mission statements. In support of this conviction about the importance of being ideologically explicit, Meg Woolbright writes, "for academic feminists, our action requires that the political circumstances in which we write and talk to students be named. In naming, we create a space in which we can talk openly about the conflicts between feminism and the patriarchy" (28). Once Writing centers establish feminist theory as a primary framework, they can begin the process of claiming the intellectual value of nurture in scholarship and in the center. However, it is not enough for scholars to claim feminist theory. They must act on it, too. As Nancy Schniedewind writes, "perhaps the greatest threat to feminism in the university is the ease with which we can allow the curriculum to reflect thought without action" (178). Moving forward, scholars can use the position of the writing center to creatively explore the practical applications of feminist theory in a learning environment—as well as the ways in which the feminist writing center can challenge the Fordist, patriarchal institution.

Works Cited

Boquet, Elizabeth H. "'Our Little Secret': A History of Writing Centers, Pre- to Post-Open Admissions." *College Composition and Communication*, vol. 50, no. 3, Feb. 1999, p. 463, https://doi.org/10.2307/358861. Accessed 15 Sept. 2019.

Brannon, Lil, and Stephen M. North. "The Uses of the Margins." *The Writing Center Journal*, vol. 20, no. 2, 2000, pp. 7–12. *JSTOR*, http://www.jstor.org/stable/43442094. Accessed 4 Jan. 2024.

Buffington, Nancy. "When Teachers Aren't Nice: bell hooks and Feminist Pedagogy." *ERIC*, 1 Mar. 1993, eric.ed.gov/?id=ED359513. Accessed 4 Jan. 2024.

Farrell, Thomas J. "The Female and Male Modes of Rhetoric." *College English*, vol. 40, no. 8, Apr. 1979, p. 909, https://doi.org/10.2307/376528. Accessed 29 Mar. 2020.

Gillespie, Paula, et al. *Writing Center Research. Routledge EBooks*, Routledge, 1 Dec. 2001. https://doi.org/10.4324/9781410604026. Accessed 4 Jan. 2024.

Grimm, Nancy Maloney. "Rearticulating the Work of the Writing Center." *College Composition and Communication*, vol. 47, no. 4, 1996, pp. 523–48. *JSTOR*, https://doi.org/10.2307/358600. Accessed 4 Jan. 2024.

Grumet, Madeleine R. *Bitter Milk: Women and Teaching*. University of Massachusetts Press, 1988. *JSTOR*, https://doi.org/10.2307/j.ctv2nhq3zp. Accessed 5 Jan. 2024.

Haltiwanger-Morrison, Talisha M., and Talia O. Nanton. "Dear Writing Centers: Black Women Speaking Silence into Language and Action." *The Peer Review*, vol. 3, no. 1, 2019. https://thepeerreview-iwca.org/issues/redefining-welcome/dear-writing-centers-black-women-speaking-silence-into-language-and-action/.

Healy, Dave. "Writing Center Directors: An Emerging Portrait of the Profession." *WPA,* vol. 18, no. 3, 1995, pp. 26-43, http://associationdatabase.co/archives/18n3/18n3healy.pdf

hooks, bell. *Yearning: Race, Gender, and Cultural Politics*. New York, Routledge, 1990.

Ianetta, Melissa, and Lauren Fitzgerald. *The Oxford Guide for Writing Tutors: Practice and Research*. Oxford University Press, 2016.

Lutes, Jean Marie. "Why Feminists Make Better Tutors: Gender and Disciplinary Expertise In a Curriculum-Based Tutoring Program." *Writing Center Research: Extending the Conversation*, 2002, pp. 235–257. https://doi.org/10.4324/9781410604026

McKinney, Jackie Grutsch (2005) "Leaving Home Sweet Home: Towards Critical Readings of Writing Center Spaces," *Writing Center Journal*: Vol. 25: Issue. 2, Article 4. DOI: https://doi.org/10.7771/2832-9414.1526.

McNamee, Kaidan, and Michelle Miley. "Writing Center as Homeplace (A Site for Radical Resistance)." *The Peer Review*, vol. 1, no. 2, 2017. https://thepeerreview-iwca.org/issues/braver-spaces/writing-center-as-homeplace-a-site-for-radical-resistance/

Miley, Michelle. "Bringing Feminist Theory Home." *Theories and Methods of Writing Center Studies*, vol. 1, 2019. https://doi.org/10.4324/9780429198755

—. "Feminist Mothering: A Theory/Practice for Writing Center Administration." *WLN*, vol. 41, no. 1, 1 Jan. 2016, pp. 17–24, https://doi.org/10.37514/wln-j.2016.41.1.04. Accessed 4 Jan. 2024.

Nanton, Talia O. and Talisha M. Haltiwanger Morrison. "Dear Writing Centers: Black Women Speaking Silence into Language and Action." *The Peer Review* 3.1, Summer 2019, https://thepeerreview-iwca.org/issues/redefining-welcome/dear-writing-centers-black-women-speaking-silence-into-language-and-action/. Accessed 13 June 2023.

Nelson, Matthew T., et al. "Making Visible the Emotional Labor of Writing Center Work." *The Things We Carry: Strategies for Recognizing and Negotiating Emotional Labor in Writing Program Administration*, edited by Courtney Adams Wooten et al., University Press of Colorado, 2020, pp. 161–76. *JSTOR*, http://www.jstor.org/stable/j.ctv180h76t.15. Accessed 4 Jan. 2024.

Nichols, Kathleen L. "A Comment on Thomas J. Farrell's 'The Female and Male Modes of Rhetoric.'" *College English*, vol. 41, no. 5, 1980, pp. 588–90. *JSTOR*, https://doi.org/10.2307/375732. Accessed 4 Jan. 2024.

North, Stephen M. "The Idea of a Writing Center." *College English*, vol. 46, no. 5, 1984, pp. 433–46. *JSTOR*, https://doi.org/10.2307/377047. Accessed 4 Jan. 2024.

O'Reilly, Andrea. *Feminist Mothering*. State University of New York Press, 2008.

Schniedewind, Nancy. "Teaching Feminist Process." *Women's Studies Quarterly*, vol. 15, no. 3/4, 1987, pp. 15–31. *JSTOR*, http://www.jstor.org/stable/40003433. Accessed 4 Jan. 2024.

Shamoon, Linda and Deborah Burns. "Labor Pains: A Political Analysis of Writing Center Tutoring." *The Politics of Writing Centers*, edited by Deborah Burns and Kathy Evertz, Boynton/Cook, 2001. https://search.worldcat.org/title/politics-of-writing-centers/oclc/46383914.

Thompson, Audrey. "For: Anti-Racist Education." *Curriculum Inquiry*, vol. 27, no. 1, 1997, pp. 7–44. *JSTOR*, http://www.jstor.org/stable/1180053. Accessed 5 Jan. 2024.

Trachsel, Mary. "Nurturant Ethics and Academic Ideals: Convergence in the Writing Center." *The Writing Center Journal*, vol. 16, no. 1, 1995, pp. 24–45. *JSTOR*, http://www.jstor.org/stable/43441986. Accessed 4 Jan. 2024.

The University of Virginia Writing Center. The Writing and Rhetoric Program. 2024, https://writingrhetoric.as.virginia.edu/welcome-writing-center. Accessed 5 Jan. 2024.

"Writing Center Philosophy." *UNT Dallas Learning Commons website*, https://www.untdallas.edu/learning/writing-center-philosophy.php. Accessed 9 June 2023.

Woolf, Virginia, and Andrew McNeillie. *The Common Reader*. First Series. Hogarth Press, 1984.

Woolbright, Meg. "The Politics of Tutoring: Feminism within the Patriarchy." *Writing Center Journal*, vol. 13, no. 1, 1 Jan. 1992, https://doi.org/10.7771/2832-9414.1276. Accessed 10 Sept. 2022.

10 The Missing Lens: The Absence of Intersectionality in Education

Saoirse Farrell

Abstract

In this paper, I explore the knowledge gaps in my pre-college education by reflecting on several readings and assignments from my Introduction to Women, Gender, and Sexuality course. The primary mode of reflection involves Krista Radcliffe's concept of rhetorical listening. Into my Radcliffe-inflected discussion of these readings, I weave the narrative of my educational experiences of textual analysis, discussing the heavy influence of Catholic school on my academic journey in college. I conclude that my K-12 education lacked an appropriate consideration of intersectionality, and I end with an urgent appeal for the inclusion of more intersectional K-12 curricula.

Introduction

When I tell people I went to Catholic school, I normally get a look of surprise and apprehension. I'm not religious anymore, and I don't fit into the image of what most think a Catholic school girl would look like—not with my crop tops emblazoned with profanities and my blunt, take-charge personality. But the truth is, I did go to Catholic school from kindergarten to 8th grade. I've only realized recently that those were some of the most formative years of my education: no matter how hard I've tried to get away from it, Catholic school has stayed with me.

It was only when I entered public school that I finally came to understand the critical gaps that my Catholic school education had left in my worldview. At public school, I encountered diversity for the first time: different religions, people open with their sexualities, people across the political spectrum, and, most visibly, a lot more people of color. I realized that most people didn't learn about the books of the Bible in Spanish class; rather, they focused on the rich cultural history of Spanish-speaking countries. I realized that, though religion provides fulfillment for many people, it can do a lot of harm as well—and Catholic school certainly harmed me. It harmed me by teaching me that gay people were going to Hell, and it harmed me by teaching me to watch the length of my skirt so that boys wouldn't get distracted. Some Catholic churches are more progressive, inclusive of the LGBTQ+ community, and less strict regarding how women and girls dress, and I know that my experience reflects the teachings of my church; others may have different, and perhaps more positive, experiences in other congregations or religions. But when I left Catholic school, I realized that it had left me with a lot to unlearn—and plenty of new things to learn about as well. However, even though I entered high school with high hopes for my journey of unlearning and learning, my attempts often left me frustrated. I didn't know where to begin, how to approach complex social issues and processes. I needed help. I needed a teacher and class time devoted to these subjects. I'm sorry to say I never got them.

Once I started college at the University of Virginia, I vowed to finally discover what Catholic school had hidden from me. Drawn to the department of Women, Gender, and Sexuality Studies (WGS), I began to take classes exploring race, women, and queer theory/history—the hallmarks of that major. My experiences in these classes confirmed my suspicions that I was missing a vast amount of information and that the concepts I was learning were vital to my developing worldview. Often, especially in my Intro to WGS class, I found myself wondering why I hadn't encountered certain concepts before. I learned about so much history that was absent from my Advanced Placement United States History course. Moving into this new learning environment, I began developing my awareness of the gaps in research due to racism, sexism, homophobia, and other forms of structural discrimination, and I wondered how my intellectual trajectory might have been different if I had learned about these topics earlier. To understand why my learning in WGS was such a revelation, I need to examine my past educational experiences—what I learned and didn't learn.

My education was designed primarily by the Archdiocese of Arlington, and secondarily by the Virginia Board of Education. For these nine years of Catholic school, I learned my fundamentals: how to read and write, how to make friends and compromise, and how to learn and investigate new ideas. Arguably, my early identity was shaped by Catholic school. Because of its uniquely designed curriculum—one marked, I now see, by forces such as institutional racism, white supremacy, sexism, and homophobia—I had a lot of gaps going into high school; unfortunately, the Virginia Board of Education, also affected by those forces, didn't quite fill those gaps.

I was missing intersectionality. I first encountered that term briefly in my first semester of college, but I learned a great deal more about the concept during my Intro to Women, Gender, and Sexuality Studies course. I now wish that I had had access to this knowledge, to the WGS frame of thinking, before college. Had I known about intersectionality and other related historical/theoretical concepts, terms that either have been systemically erased from the Virginian education system or have not yet been implemented in it, I would have become an adult with clearer eyes and gone into the world better prepared for what would greet me. While it is doubtful the concept of intersectionality itself will make it into K-12 education anytime soon, I think the framework would have made my educational experience better and more well-rounded. Indeed, I envision a future in which K-12 curriculums are inclusive and conscious of the dynamics of intersectionality. To that end, in the body of this essay, I investigate intellectual frameworks and concepts that I was taught in college but wish I had learned about earlier. I argue that the WGS framework and intersectionality are essential to students and curriculums across the U.S.

The Process of Reflection: Listening to the Past

Thoughts about my past education had been swirling in my brain for months before I gained a useful framework with which to understand those previous experiences. I originally took ENWR 3620, Writing and Tutoring Across Cultures, with the purpose of applying to work as a peer tutor at the writing center upon completion of the class, but the class has changed how I look at language, writing, and the act of reflection itself. The class investigates comparative rhetorics and the scholarship behind tutoring multilingual writers. Both during and outside of class, the course ethos encouraged writing as a method of reflecting on the readings and as a way of shaping new thoughts and ideas.

One of the articles for the class, "Rhetorical Listening: A Trope for Interpretive Invention and a 'Code of Cross-Cultural Conduct'" by Krista Ratcliffe, analyzes listening as a mode of reflection. Upon first reading, I was totally confused. Through class discussion and with help from my professor, however, I've come to understand that rhetorical listening is a way of looking beyond the text: at the author's background/identity and at the overarching power structures that govern our world, as well as at anything that is missing or unclear within the text itself. Throughout this paper, I utilize rhetorical listening, in combination with concepts from my WGS classes, to paint a clearer picture of my educational journey and development as a writer—within the context of my desires, my identity, and my world.

The Concept I Wish I Learned Earlier: Intersectionality

I called myself an intersectional feminist long before I understood what intersectionality was or the extent of its cultural significance. In high school, dimly sensing that I might identify as a feminist, I wanted to explore the concept of feminism, but I didn't have access to any guidance or instruction on this topic. My research led me to a blog—not the most reliable of sources, but, in my defense, I didn't know where to look! —which defined terms used within feminism. While writing this piece, I searched for that blog but couldn't find it. I did, however, find a comparable blog entitled "FairyGodBoss," which defines terms such as womanism, intersectionality, sexism and more (Houlis). As a budding high school feminist, I came to envision an inclusive version of feminism, one that doesn't privilege womanhood but instead considers all the identities a person may hold. I still hadn't heard of intersectionality itself as a concept utilized within feminism and other spheres, and I didn't realize that this thinking could be used as a frame for so many aspects of human society and culture. Furthermore, while I was on the right track in my developing understanding of intersectionality, I wasn't quite there yet.

When I got to college, I intended to major in history, but I wasn't passionate about pursuing the same historical narratives I had learned in high school. I looked at the course list and saw classes such as "U.S. History Before/After 1850" and was immediately bored. But then I found the perfect class: African American Women's History. For our first homework assignment, we were assigned a TedTalk by Kimberlé Crenshaw: "The Urgency of Intersectionality." Crenshaw defined a term that has ultimately shaped my thinking in everything I do, one I desperately wish I had learned earlier: intersectionality.

Intersectionality, as coined by Crenshaw, is a framework for understanding how identities overlap and create unique experiences at the sites of their intersections. The video begins with Crenshaw listing victims of police brutality and asking standing audience members to sit down once they are unfamiliar with a name. She reads the names of four men first, then the names of four women. Once Crenshaw speaks the first Black woman's name, most of the auditorium sits down. Crenshaw utilizes this exercise as a metaphor for why intersectionality is necessary. In the media and in public discourse, she demonstrates, the stories of police violence against Black men are far more visible than stories of police violence against Black women. Furthermore, while Black women experience both police violence and violence against women, the former is commonly associated with Black men and the latter with white women. Therefore, even though both police violence and violence against women make up part of Black women's experiences, society doesn't look at Black women specifically as suffering from those ills. While society often classifies these experiences as characteristic either of Blackness or of womanhood, intersectionality allows for the understanding that there are experiences unique to Black womanhood. Crenshaw furthers her explanation through the visual aid of a crossroad: one road represents race while the other represents gender identity, and Black women stand at the intersection of the two paths. As the argument of this TedTalk indicates, without intersectionality we are missing a crucial structure for thinking about social issues that will affect whether people live or die.

My understanding of intersectionality has deepened since my initial viewing of that *TedTalk*. The term has come up in multiple classes since then, many outside of the WGS department—but, more broadly, it has changed my frame of thinking. I find myself bringing intersectionality into all my classes, regardless of whether the professor mentions it first. Indeed, WGS has flipped my worldview. For example, when reviewing a syllabus for a class before college, I would look at topics and gauge my interest level. Now I look at the list of authors and ask myself what perspectives they bring to the table. Does the syllabus provide a diverse array of voices, or are the authors mainly from similar backgrounds and therefore unlikely to challenge each other? I can't ignore these kinds of questions now, and I wouldn't want to. Even outside of school, WGS has become the primary lens through which I assess the depth of wisdom that different experiences offer me. When watching movies, I can't help but analyze them within the context of what I learned during the media week of my intro course: how many people of color are featured? What type of roles do they play? Are those roles stereotypes? Are there queer characters? Is there more than one woman? Sometimes I find it a bit difficult to just watch a movie, but now my enjoyment comes more from this analysis rather than from the movie itself.

Intersectionality is the most important concept I have learned in college thus far because it allows people to get an accurate picture of the social issues affecting our society. Pervasive issues such as racism, sexism, homophobia, classism, ableism, and more affect everyone and merit continual consideration. I wish I had studied this concept earlier because intersectionality allows for the most accurate possible portrayal of how individual experiences relate to structural inequities. Throughout high school, my main areas of interest were feminism and women's rights. Because Catholic school didn't make the lens of intersectionality accessible to me, I focused on the most privileged within the women's rights movement: middle and upper class straight white women. I didn't understand the scope or complexity of the movement about which I was so passionate, and I missed out on a lot of personal development as a result.

What I Took for Granted: Gender

Before college, I never thought actively about gender. None of my health classes mentioned gender or sex, and the messaging I got was that they were one and the same. I was aware that trans people existed, but I didn't understand the relationship between gender and sex. Judith Lorber's "The Social Construction of Gender" blew open my world view by explaining the difference between gender and sex in an easily digestible manner.

Gender and sex are often constructed as connected, meaning that one is determined by the other. However, this isn't strictly true. Gender and sex assignment are distinct. Lorber principally discusses gender, but understanding sex is also important to understanding the difference between these two concepts. Sex is typically determined at birth, when a medical professional designates a person as either male or female. The determination is usually based on the physical presentation of a person's genitals, but it can also involve internal genitalia, chromosomes, hormones, etc. Sex is based on observable physical characteristics, while gender is an internal process.

Lorber argues that gender is a continuous, socially constructed process. Gender is something that I, like many others, viewed as being created at birth. In reality, gender is created by our society at every moment of every day. This creation begins as soon as we enter the world: baby girls and boys are socialized within traditional ideals of femininity and masculinity. For example, girls are often put in dresses, clothing that boys typically aren't allowed to wear. Parents dress their children in conventionally gendered ways so that society can assign them to the 'correct' group, but the construction of gender is continuous throughout our lives. Lorber posits that gender is a result of the human need for categorization and division within the labor force. Gender is constructed by society, which then privileges one gender over another—and then work is divided accordingly.

The discourse I encountered in high school only mentioned gender in relation to women's rights. Even then, discussions of women's rights surfaced in brief spurts throughout the year, gaining a superficial prominence in March during Women's History Month. We learned about Susan B. Anthony and the feminist movement in the 70s, but not much else. I thought that, once I got out of Catholic school, I would start learning about everything I missed. But I was wrong. I loved my history classes, but I was consistently disappointed when I didn't see myself in the history. Even when we did learn about women, most of them were white, and we didn't discuss their contributions as if they were equal to those of men. In general, my classmates didn't seem to mind. Whether this ambivalence stemmed from a lack of care for women or from indifference towards the subject of history itself, I couldn't say. Either way, when I read Lorber's piece, I was overjoyed. I finally understood the core ideas about gender's constructed-ness, ideas that no one in my circle had previously discussed with me. I understood that sexism stems from the unequal construction of different genders by our society, and that gender is essential to the functioning of our current society. But I wanted to know, and I still want to know: why wasn't something so essential taught earlier?

Masculinity Matters Just as Much as Femininity

In high school, I was entirely focused on women: feminism, female historical figures, femininity, attempting to fill a void. I never gave men much thought because I'd heard about them for my entire life. What I never realized was that, while society focuses on, privileges, and values men, it has largely overlooked masculinity. When taking Intro to WGS, I was skeptical about the week on masculinity. I was slightly intrigued by the concept of toxic masculinity, but it wasn't a topic that I could see myself investigating in depth. After finishing that week, masculinity was one of the aspects of my field that fascinated me most.

What changed? As part of our coursework for the week, we watched a documentary, *The Mask You Live In*. The documentary includes the definition of masculinity, an exploration of how masculinity affects other social issues, and real stories of men's experiences with masculinity. This film loosely defined masculinity as the rejection of femininity: no crying, no emotions, using violence to solve problems, economic success, sexual conquest, and athletic ability. Masculinity, in its current, dominant, American form, goes beyond simply "toxic"; it's destructive. The documentary links this version of masculinity to suicide, violence against women, homophobia, bullying, and other forms of violence.

I've heard stories about "locker room talk," in which boys speak casually about violence against women and homophobia. I can't count the number of times I've heard "that's so gay" come out of a boy's mouth. The section about homophobia explained that toxic masculinity is at fault for these casual perpetuations of discrimination. Being gay is associated with femininity, and, because masculinity instructs men to repress emotions, this combination leads to not only a rejection of gayness but also an all-too-often violent response to any form of what is perceived to be "gay." There's nothing wrong with being gay or feminine. However, queerness unsettles the foundation of masculinity on which most men in America build their identities, and, when confronted with this, men can turn violent.

While watching this film, I thought of my cousin. My sweet, fifteen-year-old cousin, who talks a lot in class and likes to read comic books, has been penalized by society in ways that I'm not able to fully comprehend. When I heard him derogatorily call something "gay," I called him out on it, calmly explaining why that's problematic and homophobic. He said he understood and acted like it wasn't a big deal; he acquiesced but brushed me off, and he has done the same thing every time I've reminded him about it since then. Because of this film, I realized he has to say it. To be considered masculine, one of the guys, he must vehemently reject everything feminine, including queerness, even when he knows what he's saying is wrong. These destructive ideas of masculinity are everywhere and affect a lot more societal issues than I thought. Masculinity can mean being courageous, a leader, a father, and more, but it can also cause harm. I never gave masculinity the space it deserves, but now I understand it better. To dismantle violence against women, homophobia, sexism, and other forms of discrimination, we must understand all constructions affecting it, including masculinity. To help dismantle structural oppression, feminist scholars need to study masculinity within an academic context, and educators need to address it in K-12 schools.

How I Fell in Love with Scholarship

The most intimidating part of college was encountering and attempting scholarly work. In high school, I kept up with the reading just fine, often finishing at a reasonable hour the night before it was due. I enjoyed it, but that quickly changed during my first year of college. My transition to college occurred during a pandemic and was decidedly rougher than most, but, whatever the cause, I just could not do the reading. My first semester, I took classes in history, international relations, religion, and poetry—all subjects that fascinate me. But the sheer number of dense pages I had to read proved to be too much, and I struggled to enjoy and digest the material. My spring semester proved to be a much better experience, and I owe my burgeoning love for scholarship to my very first WGS class.

Introduction to WGS covered topics such as intersectionality, prison reform, gender, feminism, masculinity, media, LGBTQIA+ issues, and sports. While there was traditional academic scholarship, the course also featured news articles, documentaries, and movies. It felt as if I was being eased into academia. WGS was a topic I was interested in, and I wasn't being inundated with readings. These pieces of scholarship were hard, but I began to have fun engaging with them. I found myself enjoying the articles more, finding it useful to begin with shorter readings and working my way up to longer and more dense ones. One of the most impactful pieces I read was "The Master's Tools Will Never Dismantle the Master's House" by Audre Lorde.

Lorde's essay speaks back to a conference on feminism where she was one of two Black women in attendance and the only Black lesbian featured on a panel. This reading examines the overarching, hierarchical structures that govern our society and workplaces. Lorde critiques the conference for being predominantly white and, therefore, unable to fully consider the differences between women of different races, classes, and sexualities. One of my favorite questions she asks in this piece is, "what does it mean when the tools of a racist patriarchy are used to examine the fruits of that same patriarchy?" (25). This question furthers her critique of the white feminists at the conference, asserting that, as they are formed within and privileged by the racist patriarchy of our society, they cannot accurately or fully critique the racist patriarchy. They are fruits of its labor.

Perhaps the most famous part of this essay details how resistance becomes impossible when working within an oppressive system. Lorde states, *"For the master's tools will never dismantle the master's house.* They may allow us to temporarily beat him at his own game, but they will never enable us to bring about genuine change" (27, her italics). In other words, we cannot work within a system to fully dismantle it; we are products of that system. For example, politicians, who make laws within a set system of government, are limited by the Constitution and society's constructed hierarchies, whereas activists operating outside the political system might have a better chance at making change. These ideas kept me thinking long after my class ended: how do I, as a white woman, contribute to this racist patriarchy? What can I do about it? What other tools do we have access to that can dismantle the master's house? Can we dismantle it at all? I neither agree nor disagree with Lorde's argument, but it was one of the first that led me to deeply question my beliefs and my place in society.

Lorde ends with a call to action: "I urge each one of us here to reach down into that deep place of knowledge inside herself and touch that terror and loathing of any difference that lives there. See whose face it wears. Then the personal as the political can begin to illuminate all our choices" (28). These words have inspired me to reexamine and reflect on my life and biases—something I needed and wanted to do long before I had the tools. Lorde's work helped frame other pieces of scholarship I was reading, allowing me to keep in mind the larger system at work even as I encountered articles focusing on individual elements of that system. Before college, I didn't have the language with which to begin reflecting on or understanding my experiences and internal biases. WGS gave me the gift of access to different viewpoints and the language that comes with them, but, unfortunately, not everyone can major in WGS; in fact, most people won't take a single class in the field. That's why it's essential that curriculums integrate the ideas and principles of WGS into the larger frameworks of the education system, incorporating them into all classes, especially at earlier ages.

Looking Back at a Not-So-Distant Past

I wrote my Common Application essay in the fall of 2019, during my senior year of high school, going through several drafts before settling at last on the version I submitted. This essay captures a very specific moment in time, and it is based only on the knowledge and growth I had acquired up to that point. There is only so much one can say in 650 words, but, reading those words now, I see how race, and more specifically my whiteness, comes through in my writing. I see this document as evidence of the necessity of incorporating WGS ideas and principles into high school curricula.

Names are integral to identity; they can represent a person's cultural values and the traits that connect them to human society. I began the essay with my name: "Saoirse. Ser-sha. Sear-sha. To every substitute teacher I've ever had, my name represents a conundrum." My Irish name is difficult for monolingual English speakers to pronounce, and it has been absolutely butchered by almost everyone I've ever met. My name represents the intersection of my identities, as an Irish-American "born in Dublin, Ireland on March 17, 2002, St. Patrick's Day." I wrote, "My name reflects my country of birth in that 'Saoirse' is Gaelic and has the English meaning of freedom."

While writing that essay, I never realized that my experience of having a difficult-to-pronounce name wasn't specific to Irish-American identity—that it was in fact quite common among people of different ethnicities and cultures. However, I never replaced my name with an "American name." There are some students who provide for teachers and classmates a different name, one recognizable to and easy to pronounce for English speakers. I was never forced into conformity or erased in this way. I now attribute this difference principally to race and the pressure of assimilation. Race is largely absent from my Common Application essay. For people of color, erasure of their names is common when white monolingual English speakers' standards deem those names unpronounceable. A new name for me was never in the cards, because, while my name was different, I was white, and that privilege was enough to protect me from that method of assimilation.

Throughout the essay, I detail the internal conflict between my Irish and American selves, culminating in my reclamation of "Irish-American" as an identity. A portion of my essay explains how, "when my family would visit Ireland to see my relatives during the summer, kids on the street would always tease that I sounded 'so American,' as if suggesting my American accent made me less of an Irish person […] Yet, when my family returned home from Ireland, kids made it known to me that I sounded too foreign and un-American." At one point, I even explicitly state, "I was too Irish in America and not Irish enough in Ireland." However, what I hadn't considered until I approached the topic of this paper was that this was yet again a common experience affected by race. Many mixed-race people share the feelings of not belonging to either of their cultures. While the experiences I discuss in the essay and the feelings of inner conflict that I communicate are valid, the experiences of mixed-race people are heightened and made particularly trying by a race-based alienation I do not experience. I regret that the acknowledgment of the intersection of race and identity is absent from that essay, but I want to be clear that I do not entirely blame myself.

I also blame the education system. My Catholic elementary/middle school, in combination with my Virginian public high school, failed to provide me with an education in intersectionality. I am white, and there will be experiences, particularly those of people of color, that I will not be aware of or understand upon first glance. The job of school is to educate and prepare students for the world, yet I was left woefully unprepared and undeveloped as a person. I've only realized this through taking WGS courses in college—an opportunity that is accessible to few. I was a senior in high school when I wrote this essay. I thought I understood social justice issues and was knowledgeable about politics. I was wrong, and it's clear that my Common App doesn't consider a diverse range of perspectives, merely my own, limited one. In college, I realized that there was so much I didn't know, but it would've been easier to navigate life if I had encountered WGS and similar topics earlier.

Conclusion

I talk a lot about Catholic school. Most of what I say is negative; I feel compelled to try to articulate what made it such a flawed experience. People ask if I would go back and change it if I could—would I, for example, go to public school instead? No: though I firmly believe that its curriculum needs to change, Catholic school has shaped who I am in good ways and bad, and I try not to have regrets. My education has left me with a lot of gaps to fill and unlearning to do, but, for all that, I treasure it. My passion for my discipline was born during my Catholic school years.

Not everyone in college will take a WGS-style course; indeed, not every school has access to the materials and expertise that make such a framework plausible. Furthermore, not everyone will go to college—and, even if they do, college is only four years of a person's life. What about the other thirteen years that most people spend as students? What about those who attend private Catholic school for their entire education? How can that education be more diverse? I don't have the answers to these questions, but WGS has made me realize that teachers and students need to seek and imagine curricular change—even if I don't know exactly what that should look like.

I imagine that, when I look back on this moment of introspection in a few months or even years in time, I will find holes in my analysis or new perspectives to consider, but that is okay. I'm still learning, and I look forward to discovering more about my discipline; I'm excited to explore possibilities for improvement in education. I don't know exactly what my future career path is, but I know I want to work in education. WGS has lit a fire within me, and I plan to utilize what I've learned in my future work. I want to educate people in a way that centers intersectionality and brings WGS into focus. My journey with WGS and education will continue. In the future, I hope to bring these theories and concepts to a larger audience.

Works Cited

Crenshaw, Kimberlé. "The Urgency of Intersectionality." Performance by Kimberlé Crenshaw, TED TALK, *Youtube*, 7 Dec. 2016, https://www.youtube.com/watch?v=akOe5-UsQ2o. Accessed 16 Dec. 2021.

Evans, Betsy, and Annabelle Mooney. *Language, Power, and Society*. Routledge, vol. 5, 2019.

Houlis, Anna Marie. "Feminist Terms Glossary." *Fairygodboss*, 31 Jan. 2020, https://fairygodboss.com/career-topics/feminist-terms.

Kaplan, Robert E. "Cultural Thought Patterns of Inter-Cultural Education." *Language Learning Journal*, vol. 16.1, 1966.

Ianetta, Melissa, and Lauren Fitzgerald. *The Oxford Guide for Writing Tutors: Practice and Research*. Oxford University Press, 2016.

Liu, Pei-Hsun. "A Journey of Empowerment: What Does "Better English" Mean to Me?" *TESOL, 1.3, 2010.* DOI: 10.5054/tj.2010.226927.

Lorber, Judith. "Night to His Day: The Social Construction of Gender." *Paradoxes of Gender*, Yale University Press, 1995.

Lorde, Audre. "The Master's Tools Will Never Dismantle the Master's House." 1984. *Feminist Postcolonial Theory: A Reader*. Edited by Reina Lewis and Sara Mills, Edinburgh University Press, 2003, pp. 25-8.

Mori, Kyoko. *Polite Lies: On Being a Woman Caught between Cultures*, Ballantine 1999.

Newsom, Jennifer Siebel, et al. *The Mask You Live In*. The Representation Project, 2015, https://therepproject.org/product/the-mask-you-live-in-curriculum-its-always-free/

Olson, Bobbi. "Rethinking Our Work with Multilingual Writers: The Ethics and Responsibility of Language Teaching in the Writing Center." *Praxis*, vol. 2, 1 Jan. 2013, https://doi.org/10.15781/t2g15tt1t. Accessed 4 Jan. 2024.

Phillipson, Robert. "Linguistic Imperialism" *Blackwell Publishing Ltd.,* 2013. The Encyclopedia of Applied Linguistics, DOI: 10.1002/9781405198431.wbeal0718.

Ratcliffe, Krista. "Rhetorical Listening: A Trope for Interpretive Invention and a 'Code of Cross-Cultural Conduct.'" *College Composition and Communication,* vol. 51, no. 2, 1999, p. 195, https://doi.org/10.2307/359039.

Rodríguez, Richard. "Aria: A Memoir of a Bilingual Childhood*.: Semantic Scholar.*" 1980, http://mrbeland.weebly.com/uploads/3/0/5/5/30558007/aria.pdf.

Severino, Carol. "Crossing Cultures with International ESL Writers: The Tutor as Contact Zone Contact Person." *A Tutor's Guide: Helping Writers One-To-One,* vol. 2. Heinemann, 2005.

Severino, Carol. "The Sociopolitical Implications of Response to Second Language and Second Dialect Writing." *Journal of Second Language Writing,* vol. 2, no. 3, Sept. 1993, pp. 181–201, https://doi.org/10.1016/1060-3743(93)90018-x. Accessed 17 Sept. 2020.

Tan, Amy. "Mother Tongue." *Threepenny Review,* no. 34, 1990, 7-8. JSTOR, https://www.jstor.org/stable/4383908.

Young, Vershawn A. "'Naw, We Straight:' An Argument Against Code Switching." *JAC,* vol. 29, no. 1/2, 2009, 49-76. JSTOR, https://www.jstor.org/stable/20866886.

11 Clara Luz

Susan Gonzalez Guevara

Human migration has occurred for approximately two million years. During that time, different groups of people have migrated for different reasons, including "push" and "pull factors." Push factors involve the countries people are trying to leave—for instance, poverty, corrupt governments, and war. Pull factors include ideas or conditions that attract people to a different country, making them want to migrate—for instance, opportunities for work, government assistance, and better living conditions.

Seventeen years ago, my mom faced several factors, both push and pull, that led her to migrate from Guatemala to the United States. She left the only place she had ever called home, and she decided to bring me with her. I was three years old. Not only did she struggle to get to this country, but, once she arrived, she also experienced what it was like to be uneducated in a country where education was, and continues to be, a necessity. Her experience as an uneducated immigrant in the U.S. is one that I feel is worth sharing.

While my mom faced many difficulties in coming to this country, I, too, faced my own numerous obstacles growing up as an immigrant child. In the U.S, one in ten children who are U.S. citizens live in mixed-status families. Living with someone with undocumented status (also known as mixed status) can have dramatic effects on a child's journey and identity. Furthermore, these effects are usually misunderstood due to widespread false narratives. I hope that sharing my mom's story and my experiences will help educate people and promote interest in the subject of immigration.

In the fall of my sophomore year, I took a class called "Writing and Tutoring Across Cultures," which included a weekly tutoring component. I was excited to take this class because I was going to be able to work with LAMA (Latinx and Migrant Aid), an organization in the Charlottesville community. I always enjoy helping my community, and being able to help migrants is especially important to me. In this essay, I will describe the work I did with those individuals, and I will explain some of the similarities I noticed between their stories and my mom's experience.

One last but very important idea I want to emphasize is that part of this history is not my own. I will be sharing a story that belongs to my mom, and I will be doing so with her permission, in the hope that it will help others to understand the struggles of the migrant community. Sharing the stories of others is common, but it is important to understand that these individuals are not voiceless. Immigrants of all statuses do not need others to speak for them, but we can help their stories to be heard. Simply by being better informed about the struggles of the migrant community, we can promote more substantive, helpful engagement with the issues that affect migrants.

"Todas las mañanas iba a traer agua para la casa."

The sound of the roosters woke everyone in the village. My mom woke up and made her way down the dirt path leading to what I imagine to be a well. It took her half an hour to get there, and, if she was lucky, there was no one else waiting to get water for their own home. Once the buckets were full, she wrapped her small hands around the handles and made her way up the hill until she saw the mint green house. Like most houses in the village, the mint green house had no windows or doors, just rectangular holes allowing in a fresh breeze and some light. Throughout the village, roofs were large metal slabs which didn't always cover the whole house. Open roofs were a problem when it rained—but rainy days were good days for my mom. When people felt the droplets, they rushed to place buckets, bowls, and empty plastic bottles outside, to try and collect water. If all the buckets were full, my mom wouldn't have to walk for water the next morning.

Every morning, rain or shine, my mother heated the water and made coffee for her parents and her five younger siblings. At the same time, her older sister was making tortillas for the family. Her father ate first, and, as soon as he finished, he walked to the fields. While everyone was finishing up, my mother started to clean—and tried to find time to eat her own breakfast. She helped her siblings get ready for school; they usually walked together. After classes, they all walked back, making multiple stops on the way home. Sometimes they bought eggs or milk from a corner store that was just someone's house with a bunch of products from their farm. On occasion, her older sister couldn't make tortillas, so they purchased them from a lady by the dirt path. It was always my mom's responsibility to figure out what her siblings and parents were going to eat for dinner. What was my grandma doing while my mom took care of so many things in the house?

Mi mamá nunca pudo cuidar a sus hijos. Tenía muchos y los seguía teniendo como sí tenía el dinero para mantenerlos. Hubo un tiempo que mejor se deprimio y nos dejaba solos, habiendo que haciamos. No se preocupaba por si íbamos a la escuela o si comíamos. Todos mis hermanos me pedían las cosas a mi. Pero llegó un tiempo que ya no podía ni enfocarme a lo mío, y es cuando mejor deje de ir a las escuela.

[My mom was never able to take care of her children. She had so many, and she kept having them as if she had the money to support them. There was a time when she got depressed and left us alone to fend for ourselves. She did not worry about whether we went to school or whether we ate. All my siblings asked me for things instead of her. But there came a time when I could not focus on myself, and it got to the point that I had to stop going to school.]

Eventually, as my grandma kept having more kids, my mother's routine fell apart. She sometimes missed school to take care of her newborn siblings. Before the youngest could even walk, my grandma was pregnant again. The last time she was pregnant, she had twins. Although everyone was excited by the idea of identical twins in the family, my mom wondered how they were going to afford to take care of an even larger family. By this time, there were eleven siblings total. When she was eleven years old, my mother was no longer able to keep up with school.

In Guatemala, the public school system was—and continues to be—completely broken. Unlike in the U.S., no one went searching for my mom when she started missing so much school or even when she dropped out completely. Due to the levels of poverty and certain cultural beliefs, this problem is common in several countries in Latin America. Some parents cannot afford to take time off to care for their younger children, so they count on their older children to care for them. Lack of transportation and the responsibility of making money also prevent kids from going to school; a lack of jobs worsens the effects of poverty. My mother faced difficulty getting a job in the fields because she was a woman. So, she took the role of a caretaker until her siblings were old enough to care for themselves.

Although my mom made several sacrifices for me, I found myself making some as well—especially as I got ready to go to college.

For years, I was under the impression that I would not be able to attend college. As a low-income student who was not eligible for any government aid, I was sure that I was headed for community college. I would be able to stay home and work, which would save a lot of money. Fortunately, I got into the University of Virginia. At the time, I was not sure how much it would cost to attend, but several people assured me that the school's financial aid would be one of my best options. I was excited by the thought of going away for college, which had never seemed possible until that moment. I waited all summer to receive my financial aid offer from the university and never got it. However, the university decided that, due to Covid, coming to campus would be optional. Eager to live the experience fully, I wanted to go to campus—but my mom and life had other plans.

My mom had stopped working due to Covid, so she and my sister asked if I would consider staying home and working. Because of Covid, my sister had also started working shorter hours, and they thought having a little more income would help pay a bill or two. In mixed-status households, it is common for young people to feel a sense of responsibility for our families; in my case, with limited work opportunities, being able to help financially at home was important. When my mom and sister proposed their idea, I told them that, of course, if it was possible, I would stay. Another common problem among children in mixed-status households is guilt for being able to move forward in life and leave others behind. That was exactly how I felt when I got into the university and thought I was going to have to leave, and the new plan assuaged some of that guilt. Furthermore, I still had not received my financial aid, so, since staying home would negate room and board, it made logical sense to stay home for the first semester of college.

My first semester of college was an experience I hope never to relive. I had developed a distaste for attending virtual classes—and especially for trying to navigate the technical difficulties that inevitably crop up in them—when I did it during the last couple of months of high school. Being in a small apartment (where my niece also attended class virtually, my four-year-old nephew played with his toys, and my mom watched TV) made it even more difficult. I decided to watch recorded lectures for the classes that had that option, but, because I worked so much, I never actually watched those recorded lectures. As I missed some assignments and rushed through others, I fell behind in several classes. Increasingly, I felt that work was taking up all my time. My mom never explicitly asked me to work so many hours; she just suggested that it would be helpful and financially smart to stay home, and a sense of responsibility made me feel that I should work as much as I could. I was not putting in enough time or effort into my classes, and, at some point, I no longer felt like a college student.

By the end of the semester, I did not feel like someone who had just finished her first semester of college. There was one class that I was required to attend, which was probably the only class I got anything out of. By that time, I had received my financial aid from the university, so I knew that the best thing was to move to campus for the following semester. My mom always told me that school came first, so I knew she would be okay with my decision. However, I knew that, if I had stayed home, she would have appreciated it. I have made a lot of tough decisions, but leaving my family to go to college in-person during a pandemic was a particularly momentous one. I still do not know if it was the right one.

Being away from home and unable to help gave me a lot of anxiety. Although I did better academically during my second semester, I felt less productive because I was not working. I had lost my sense of time. I found myself awake all night and taking long naps throughout the day. I would take any opportunity to go home. I had a really hard time adjusting to being just a student. I had been a working student for so long that, without the need to balance those two lifestyles, I fell out of my usual patterns.

In Guatemala, it is common for women to get married very young. Some get married and have children as early as thirteen. My mom, on the other hand, waited until her youngest sibling was about six years old. At twenty-one, she married my dad, Luis Gonzalez, a man who lived in a nearby village. She had their first child, my sister, a year later. They stayed in my mom's village because my mom wanted to continue helping my grandma, especially since some of her siblings had decided to migrate to the U.S. The living conditions in Guatemala were not getting any better; a lack of jobs was causing a large amount of people to leave the country. Worried for the financial stability of his family, my dad decided to go to the U.S. for a couple of years to earn some money. At the time, my sister was eight years old, and I was not even in the picture yet.

His idea made a lot of sense to my mom. She thought he would go there, work, and send money back. It was and continues to be common for people to migrate and send money back to their loved ones in their home country. A lot of Central American immigrants live very simple lives in the U.S., and sometimes people migrate and save money for years until they are ready to retire to their home country. However, after a couple months, my mom realized that, with my father, this was not the case.

> *Tu papá lo que fue a ganar fue un vicio. Nunca me mandó dinero porque todo se lo gastaba en andar tomando. Se vino más de cinco años a los Estados Unidos y cuando regresó a Guatemala no traía ni un dólar. Lo único que regresó fue una adicción que lo fue matando y finalmente arruinó nuestra familia.*
> [What your dad gained was an addiction. He never sent me money because he spent it all on drinking. He came to the U.S. for more than five years, and, when he returned to Guatemala, he did not bring with him a single dollar. The only thing he brought back was an addiction that was killing him and destroying our family.]

In May of 2005, my mom made the decision to leave the only place she had ever called home. My dad's addiction to alcohol drove him to become violent. She had had a child and wanted to get as far away from the violence as possible. She also had several younger siblings who had established their lives and families in the U.S. Once they found out about her situation, they agreed to help her move, telling her how great it would be for me to go to school there. Although my sister was getting a decent education in Guatemala, they were sure that there would be additional opportunities for me if I grew up in the U.S. It was obvious that the public school system in Guatemala was failing, so private school was much more effective; my sister's education was decent because it was being paid for by my mom's siblings who lived in the U.S. After some reassurance, my mom was convinced that the best thing to do for my future was to migrate. And that is exactly what she did.

The idea was that she would take me and my sister without my dad noticing. The only issue was that my sister refused to go. She was a teenager, and my mom understood that she had established friendships; at the time, she also had a great relationship with our dad. My mom decided to leave her in Guatemala—but soon realized that this was a mistake.

Having found out that my mom had left the country with one of his daughters, my dad was extremely angry. He ended up directing his anger towards my sister. He called her a liar and a traitor for not telling him that we were leaving. The behavior escalated to the point that my sister had to move out and live with another family member. This was the first and most immediate regret my mom had about leaving.

She later understood that she might never see her other daughter or her mom again.

Her early responsibilities in taking care of her siblings were only the beginning of a pattern that would continue to define—and dominate—my mom's life through adulthood. Unable to find a job when she first came to the United States, she took care of her brother's kids. This was a practical agreement since we were going to be living in his house; moreover, my mom knew no English and lacked work authorization.

Taking care of three toddlers and an infant was only part of my mother's new set of responsibilities. She was also in charge of household duties like cooking and cleaning. So, again, she would wake before the sun came up; now, though, she woke to the sound of an alarm. She prepared and bagged lunches for her three brothers before they left for work at 5 AM. She made breakfast for all the kids and woke us all up soon after. One by one, she helped us shower and get dressed. Unlike at her childhood home, however, we ate breakfast all together, herself included. These were the moments that helped my mom realize that she had made the right decision in coming to the United States. She knew that my life would be different, just as she had hoped.

Cuando ustedes eran niños pudieron disfrutar. Tienen tantos juguetes y como eran de casi la misma edad se agarraban bien. Siempre los llevamos al parque o a la piscina. Nos íbamos de compras y a veces los llevaba en las bicicletas porque no querían caminar. Y yo que ni usar una bicicleta puedo… Cuando yo era niña no había dinero para comprar cosas asi. Imaginate que si mi papá me compraba una a mi le tocaba comprar uno para todos y simplemente no teníamos el dinero ni para uno.

[When you and your cousins were children, you were able to enjoy life. You guys had so many toys, and, since you were close in age, you got along so well. We would always take you to the park or to the pool. We would go shopping, and sometimes I would take you guys on your bikes because you refused to walk. Imagine that; I could not even use a bike. When I was a child, there was no money to buy things like that. Imagine, if my dad bought me one, he would have had to buy one for all my siblings, and we simply did not have the money for that.]

Eventually, my cousins and I started going to school. For the first time in her life, my mom had a couple hours in which to relax. However, her living situation never allowed her to use that time to work on herself; she knew she needed to learn English, but her commitment to taking care of her nieces and nephew stood in the way.

Two years after we came to the U.S., my uncle, with whom we were living, was deported back to Guatemala. This caught everyone by surprise because he had been in the U.S. the longest and was married to a U.S. citizen. My aunt and cousins had a hard time accepting that their beloved family member was in Guatemala and could not come home, and my mom was completely distraught and shaken with fear. No one in my family had ever been deported, and the fact that my uncle was married to a U.S. citizen made his deportation especially hard to comprehend. However, now that I know more about immigration, I know that family-sponsored immigration is a long and costly process—which could explain why they were able to deport my uncle.

This event and its many ramifications comprise another example of how being in a mixed-status family can greatly impact everyone involved. Although my cousins and their mom were U.S. citizens, the fact that their father's life was upended by immigration laws also affected them. They lost their primary source of income and half of their emotional support. During this time, my mom recalls my two eldest cousins doing poorly in elementary school. One of the biggest changes was in their behavior: they became violent in school.

Shortly after my uncle's deportation, my dad passed away. Just as my mom had predicted, alcoholism killed him. At the time, I was only five years old, and no one told me that he had passed away. I never have a lot to say about him because I do not remember him, but my mom and sister do.

Era buen hombre pero tristemente no pudo controlar el vicio. El siempre decía que me odiaba porque te traje a este país pero él no sabía que lo mejor para ti era que estuvieras aquí. Cuando se murió todo mundo me quiso culpar a mi, especialmente la familia de él. Que porque yo me vine de Guatemala él se puso triste y alcohólico. Pero no sabían que antes de eso él ya era alcohólico. Me hace triste porque sé que la vida sin papa es difícil para ustedes.

[He was a good man, but sadly he could not control his addiction. He always said that he hated me because I brought you to this country, but he did not know that what was best for you was to be here in the U.S. When he passed away, everyone wanted to blame me, especially his family. They said that he got sad because I left Guatemala and that was what drove him to become an alcoholic. But they did not know that he was an alcoholic before that. It makes me sad because I know that life without a dad is difficult for both of you.]

My sister came to the U.S. four years after my mom and I did. When she got married and had her first child, we thought it would be a good idea to live together. Eventually, I had to dedicate time to taking care of my niece—just like my mother had. As much as my mom tried to give me a better and easier life, it was not as easy as she hoped.

We moved into a one-bedroom apartment on a street known as "Commerce." It was a busy street close to the interstate, and the apartment complex stretched an entire block. On one side, there was a shopping plaza; the apartments were on the other side. Each building looked the same, with four floors and eight balconies facing the street. It was strange that, if I told someone "I live on Commerce Street," they knew exactly where I lived, but I found a sense of community there. Commerce Street was made up predominantly of Central American immigrant families. Although the living conditions were better when we lived with my uncle in his house, I felt as if I was able to connect with people who understood me. I did not grow up knowing what it meant for me to be an immigrant; it was this community that helped me realize how many obstacles I would come to face.

When I was eleven years old, I walked to school like all the other kids who lived on my street. The difference between me and all those kids was that I had to be home after school, no matter what. After school, everyone would drop off their bookbags, put on their play shoes, and go to the park at the end of the street. At that time, all the adults in my house were working. My niece's babysitter charged by the hour, so, to save money, my sister asked that I pick her up after school. We lived four buildings away from the babysitter, so, every day after school, I picked her up and then walked her back to our apartment. I remember my mom and sister telling me never to open the door for anyone. I always thought this was for safety reasons, but now I think they were more concerned with people questioning why an eleven-year-old and a three-month-old were home alone.

When I did my volunteering with LAMA during the fall of my sophomore year, I heard stories like my mom's. I was assigned to work with Sin Barreras, which is an organization that provides support and education opportunities for the immigrant community in Charlottesville and the surrounding area. I worked specifically with a group of adults who had some schooling in their home country and wanted to continue to learn so that they could take the GED test. I understood where most of these individuals were coming from, and I realized that my mom could easily have joined this group since she, too, had some education but never was able to finish. When I sat down and talked with people from this group, when I listened as they shared some of their experiences, I saw not only the patterns among their reasons for ceasing to attend school but also the effect that a lack of general education was having on their everyday lives. I saw in them what I always saw in my mom: fear. Like my mom, they came to the U.S. to find jobs and raise their children. They knew that there would be better opportunities in this country, but they were also trying to learn a new language and adapt to a new culture, a culture in which knowing how to write and read is a necessity.

There was something specific that stood out to me: growing up, I knew that my mom could not write, and she claimed that she just never learned how. Because I knew she attended some school and had to have learned how to write at least in part, I asked her again about her history with writing.

> *Si, aprendí cómo escribir todas las letras pero no cómo se escribe todas las palabras. Además yo no pasaba escribiendo afuera de la escuela entonces como que se me fue olvidando. Cuando llegue a los Estados Unidos me tocó recordar pero igual no me salen todas bien. Pero la gente me entiende.*

[Yes, I learned how to write all the letters but not how to write all the words. In addition, I did not spend much time writing outside of school, so I started to forget how to write. When I came to the United States, I had to remember, but sometimes it still does not work out for me. But people still understand me.]

For years, I had been under the impression that my mom was not taught to write because she was not able to get far enough in school. However, I discovered that the reason for her backwards "e" and use of only upper case "L" was that, though she did learn to write in school, she never practiced writing and eventually forgot some of the basics. Many children practice writing almost every day because it is an everyday life skill. In villages in Guatemala, writing was not often necessary; it wasn't a quotidian skill that enabled mastery through frequent use—which explains why my mom doesn't know how to write.

At my tutoring site, I saw a woman struggling in a way that reminded me of my mom. The woman was much older than the other tutees, and I noticed that she was having trouble writing. Her letters were large; she brought intense focus to the act of writing and progressed more slowly than everyone else did. I asked her if she needed any help. I had always liked how everyone in the group was able to feel comfortable talking to each other, and I was relieved that she was able to open up to me. She told me that she just did not write that often, so she forgot how to write certain things. I told her how my mom had told me the same thing before and that, if she kept practicing, it would come back. Seeing these similarities among different members of the migrant community reminds me of how connected we really are. We all experience culture shock, and adapting is even harder for those who migrate at an older age.

I think the students in the GED class enjoyed having a tutor who understood them. Not only did I understand why this individual could not write, but I also accepted it and knew how common it was. I also understood why the people I met at the tutoring site were trying to get their GED. Education in the U.S. is so essential, but there's a common misconception that only immigrant youth can take advantage of that cultural and economic reality. All immigrants can benefit from educational opportunities in their new country. Learning the language and culture is essential for building a successful life in the place they are trying to make their home.

Growing up, I never thought about the negative impact that my mom's lack of education had on her. I never wondered why she wasn't able to write or read anything beyond basic Spanish; I just accepted that that was normal for her. As soon as I was able to read, I did my best to translate for her. When I first started going to school, I could only read in English, so I tried to find the right way to explain documents or letters to her in Spanish. As I got older, I learned how to read in Spanish, and I read aloud the parts that I found important. As my English got better, my mother started asking me to fill out my own school forms—and then our doctor forms. I learned how to pay bills, write checks, and properly send mail before I had my first paying job.

To this day, my mother still asks me to pretend to be her on the phone because she does not want to risk not being understood. More recently, because I left for college, I have been showing her how to do things without having to call. For example, I helped her set up mobile banking, so she did not have to call the bank anymore. When she must pay bills, she usually still calls me for help, but I am okay with that.

Once, sitting at my tutoring site, I overheard some students discussing the things they hoped to do after learning how to properly write and read. They talked about applying for jobs, writing a resume, taking their driver's license test, communicating with their children's teachers, and many other life tasks. The conversation made me wonder how much my mom struggled when she first came to this country. She never had the opportunity to achieve any of the milestones to which they aspired. She never filled out a resume because she was always busy caring for others; she never took her driver's license test because she never learned to drive. Political discourse focuses on immigrants' struggles for human rights but overlooks all the simple things they are not able to do, like applying for a job and driving. But I have always known—and my experience tutoring has confirmed—that there is a community that struggles to do those things.

I was fortunate to come to this country at a young age. Just as my uncles had predicted, I got a better education and more opportunities than I would have had in Guatemala. The only person I can thank for the life I have today is my mom. She made so many sacrifices, including leaving her family, knowing that she might never see them again. She knew that she could not provide me with the best life in the U.S., but she did enable me to succeed. She put all her time into helping create the person I am today. I hope that, once I graduate college and can live independently, she will be able to return to Guatemala, just as she has always dreamed.

Contributor Biographies

Melissa Abel is a fourth-year student at the University of Virginia pursuing a Bachelor of Arts degree in both Spanish and Cognitive Science with a concentration in Cognitive Psychology. Melissa is a research assistant in the Developmental Neuroanalytics Lab studying early social development at the UVA NICU. She is also a passionate member of the Cavalier Marching Band and has served in a variety of volunteer roles during her time at the University including interpreting at the hospital, dog walking at the SPCA, and serving as a medical assistant at the Charlottesville Free Clinic. She hopes to continue exploring the intersections of her language skills with medicine as she applies to medical school, eventually hoping to become a neonatologist.

Kaitlyn Baker is a third-year student at the University of Virginia pursuing a Bachelor of Arts degree in history with a concentration in law and society. She is active in community mobilization, serving as Vice President of Planned Parenthood Generation Action at the University of Virginia and a fellow at Planned Parenthood South Atlantic. Passionate about exploring the ways in which the law can be used to uplift and benefit marginalized communities, she also works as a legal intern and attorney liaison at the Free Legal Clinic hosted by the Maxine Platzer Lynn Women's Center at the University of Virginia. In the writing world, she is an editor at the Virginia Undergraduate Law Review and has worked as an editor on *The Lived Experience of Democracy,* published by New City Community Press. After she graduates in 2023, Kaitlyn intends to pursue a Juris Doctor degree and to begin work as an estate planning attorney.

Thaqeb Chowdhury is a graduate from the University of Virginia with a Bachelor of Arts degree in Economics and a minor in Statistics. During his time as a student, Thaqeb volunteered with Campus Kitchens to distribute meals to homeless shelters throughout Charlottesville. He worked to fund events where creative youths could express themselves through the art of spoken word and poetry as the Finance Chair for FLUX at UVA. He now works as a data specialist, connecting his passions in analytics and writing to craft engaging stories and insights for clients.

Saoirse Farrell is a third-year at the University of Virginia pursuing a major in Women, Gender, and Sexuality Studies and a double minor in Government and Global Studies in Education. At UVA, Saoirse is a Resident Advisor with Housing and Residence Life where she works to support and create inclusive communities for first year students. She is interested broadly in the field of education, including teaching and bringing her major to areas of education policy. After graduation, Saoirse hopes to further her education by pursuing a Gender Studies Master's Degree.

Susan Gonzalez is a third-year at the University of Virginia majoring in Media Studies with a minor in Sociology. She has always had a passion for advocating for the undocu+ community at the university and in the broader community. Since her first year at UVA, she has been involved with the organization undocUVa on Grounds. During her third year, she served as one of the co-vice presidents of undocUVa. One of her long-term goals is for the institution to be a more inclusive and supportive space for undocu+ students. Working with Sin Barreras allowed her to get involved with the immigrant and Latinx communities in Charlottesville.

Caitlin Gerrard is a fourth-year at the University of Virginia majoring in English and minoring in Chinese. During her third year, she enrolled in Writing and Tutoring Across Cultures with Professor Kostelnik which led her to explore ELL tutoring opportunities in the Charlottesville area. Alongside her interest in teaching, Caitlin is interested in digital humanities and is involved with the Digital Production Group of the University Library.

Quenby Hersh is a graduate student in the English department at the University of Virginia, where she teaches first-year writing. She studies nineteenth- and twentieth-century British literature and culture with specific interest in aesthetic theory, reading processes, affective resonance, and writing pedagogy. She is currently working toward finishing a thesis centered on Vernon Lee's understanding of *Einfülung*, or empathy, and its relation to her psychological aesthetics and literary criticism. Quenby earned her BA in English from Columbia University in 2021.

Kate Kostelnik is an associate professor of Writing and Rhetoric at the University of Virginia. Her fiction, which earned a 2007 fellowship from the New Jersey State Council on the Arts, has appeared in *Hayden's Ferry* and *Fifth Wednesday Journal*, among other venues. Her scholarship has been published in *Creative Writing: Teaching, Theory, and Practice*; *The Fiction Writers Review*; and *Pedagogy*. Her work in collections include a discussion of the intersections between creative writing pedagogy and writing center theory in *Creative Writing Pedagogies for the 21st Century* (SIUP) and an argument for the incorporation of literature and imaginative writing in First-Year Composition in the collection *Changing Creative Writing in America* (NCTE). At UVA she teaches first-year English and writing (ENWR) courses that combine multiple aspects of English studies. She also teaches community-engaged, literature, and upper-level pedagogy courses that ask what it means to communicate and learn across cultures.

Hannah Loeb is an English PhD candidate at the University of Virginia, where she is writing a dissertation about the spectral haunting of iambic pentameter in contemporary free verse contexts. Hannah earned her BA in English from Yale University in 2012 and her poetry MFA from the Iowa Writers' Workshop in 2015. Her poetry has appeared in *Booth*, *The Moth*, *Oxford Poetry*, *Ninth Letter*, and elsewhere. Hannah spent four years as a high school English teacher in Chile and Idaho, and, at UVa, she has worked as a peer mentor for other grad student writing instructors.

Ahmed Mohamed is a graduate of the University of Virginia with a Bachelor of Arts degree in Cognitive Science. As an undergraduate student, Ahmed was involved with the refugee community in Charlottesville, helping tutor young Arabic-speaking students and translating documents at the local food pantry. Ahmed also spent his time doing research and volunteering at the UVA Medical Center. He is now a second-year medical student.

Mariam Mohamed is a recent graduate of the University of Virginia obtaining her Bachelor of Science degree in Communication Sciences and Disorders. Throughout her time at the University of Virginia, Mariam tutored in local elementary and middle schools, as well as worked at the university's student disability center (SDAC) to provide accessible texts for blind and hard-of-seeing individuals. She also minored in Global Studies in Education as she loves learning about how to best communicate with and teach a wide range of diverse populations. Mariam is now a first year Doctorate of Audiology student at JMU hoping to become an audiologist and a professor down the road.

Casey Ocasal is completing her MA in English as part of a 4+1 program at the University of Virginia, where she graduated in 2023 with a B.A. in English (Highest Distinction). She completed Writing and Tutoring Across Cultures during the Spring of 2021 and worked in the UVa Writing Center from 2021-2023.

Kirsty Thompson is a recent graduate of the University of Virginia obtaining her Bachelor of Science degree in Communication Sciences and Disorders with a minor in Spanish. While at UVA, Kirsty was a Research Assistant for two labs, the SCHOOL (Social Confounders for Health Outcomes Linked to Education) Project and the Imaging & Communication Outcomes Lab. She also served as the Head Program Director of CLASS (Creative Learning After School & Summer) for Madison House, worked as a UVA Writing Center Tutor, interned with A1 Language, and studied abroad in Valencia, Spain. She is now a graduate student at JMU pursuing her Master's in Speech Language Pathology to become a Speech Language Pathologist.

Tanvika Vegiraju is a third-year student at the University of Virginia pursuing a major in Neuroscience and English. Throughout all her years on Grounds, she has volunteered with VISAS, a program in which she has tutored and UVA international students and staff. Her interest in this work led her to enroll in Writing and Tutoring Across Cultures with Professor Kostelnik, where she furthered her knowledge on skills and knowledge about intercultural communication. She hopes to incorporate teaching and mentoring to diverse audiences into her future career.

www.ingramcontent.com/pod-product-compliance
Lightning Source LLC
Chambersburg PA
CBHW020333170426
43200CB00006B/370